M000026212

Advance praise for

An Army of Ex-Lovers

"Part social history, part personal memoir, and part off-beat love story. Amy Hoffman writes with so much charm and wit that this portrait of a group of political radicals trying to change the world becomes an endearing and completely accessible tribute to the power of community and the importance of convictions. There is something to love, admire, and laugh about on every page of this book. I hated to see it end."

—Stephen McCauley, author of *The Object of My Affection*

"*An Army of Ex-Lovers* is Amy Hoffman's witty, nuanced, personal history of *Gay Community News*, Boston's gay weekly newspaper in the 1970s and '80s. I expected as much from this fine writer. What is delightfully unexpected is that it is also the love story between a gay man and a lesbian. Political, cranky, fully committed, loyal, and loud. It's big love. It's the untold story of those early years of gay liberation."

—Kate Clinton, author of *Don't Get Me Started*

An Army of Ex-Lovers

So much love,

Amy

AN ARMY OF EX-LOVERS

My Life at the *Gay Community News*

Amy Hoffman

University of Massachusetts Press *Amherst*

Copyright © 2007 by Amy Hoffman

All rights reserved
Printed in the United States of America

LC 2007020204
ISBN 978-1-55849-621-7 (pbk. : alk. paper)
ISBN 978-1-55849-620-0 (cloth : alk. paper)

Designed by Sally Nichols
Set in Monotype Bell
Printed and bound by The Maple-Vail Book Manufacturing Group

Library of Congress Cataloging-in-Publication Data

Hoffman, Amy.
An army of ex-lovers : my life at the Gay Community News / Amy Hoffman.
p. cm.
Includes bibliographical references and index.
ISBN 978-1-55849-621-7 (pbk. : alk. paper) — ISBN 978-1-55849-620-0
(cloth : alk. paper)
1. Hoffman, Amy. 2. Lesbians—Massachusetts—Boston—Biography. 3. Women
newspaper editors—Massachusetts—Boston—Biography. 4. Newspaper editors—
Massachusetts—Boston—Biography. 5. Gay press—Massachusetts—Boston. 6.
Gay Community News (Boston, Mass.) 7. Gay liberation movement. I. Title.
HQ75.4.H65A3 2007
306.76'63092—dc22
[B]
2007020204

British Library Cataloguing in Publication data are available.

For Richard

An army of lovers cannot fail.
  —gay liberation slogan

CONTENTS

CONTENTS

x

Illustrations follow page 86

INTRODUCTION

In October 1978, I climbed the stairs to the *Gay Community News* office, and my life changed forever. A shy, idealistic twenty-six-year-old, I encountered a group of politically committed, charismatic eccentrics, some of whom would become my "gay family" for the rest of my life.

Gay Community News was founded in June 1973 at the Charles Street Meetinghouse—a Unitarian Universalist church and community center that hosted a coffeehouse and a program for gay youth in Boston's Beacon Hill, the city's gay neighborhood. David Peterson, one of *GCN*'s founders—an MIT graduate who took every opportunity to dress up as a nun, Sister Mary Apathy, and who eventually became my landlord—used to reminisce about having to climb through a window in the kitchen to get to the mimeograph machine. (In the way of these things, the meetinghouse is now an indoor mall with a flower shop and an ice cream stand for the tourists. Beacon Hill has not been a gay neighborhood for decades; the gay men have all moved to the South End.)

After the Stonewall Riots in New York, in 1969, Boston had become a national center of gay organizing, teeming with activists, many of them veterans of the antiwar and feminist movements. (When New York City police stormed into the Stonewall bar in Greenwich Village, the patrons, many of whom were drag queens, rioted for three days rather than pile into the police vans as they usually did. Although gay and lesbian rights organizations existed before June 1969, the riots, still commemorated by pride marches around the world each spring, mark the beginning of a gay liberation movement whose slogans were "Come out" and "We are

GCN's *Stonewall tenth anniversary issue, showing a plaque repeatedly posted by activists at the site of the riots and removed by the building's owner.*

everywhere.") So many new gay organizations were springing up, and they wanted to do so many different kinds of activities—lobby for a gay rights bill, organize a gay men's child-care collective, produce plays and concerts, run lesbian dances, go hiking in the White Mountains—that they needed a way to keep in touch with each other. *Gay Community News* started with fairly modest ambitions, but almost immediately evolved from a mimeographed event listing into a full-fledged weekly newspaper with offices on the second floor of 22 Bromfield Street in the heart of downtown Boston.

Nobody on the paper had any journalism experience, but that was only a minor obstacle. Organized as a collective, the members would learn whatever they needed to know as they went along. Besides news, editorials, readers' letters, and op-ed essays (when an article was attacked from all sides, the staff knew they had done a good job), *GCN* published reviews of gay films, books, plays, and concerts (there were few enough of these that we could cover them all), humor and parody, personal stories, profiles, interviews, gay history and political analysis, gossip, comic strips, crossword puzzles, and probably even a recipe or two. One of its first columns, Odyssey of a Unicorn, chronicled the daily lives of *GCN*'s classified advertising manager, Nancy Walker, and her closeted significant other, "Sother," and made Nancy into a nationally beloved figure. Nancy could wring several weeks of stories out of an episode of car trouble or the illness of her pet turtle, her subtext apparently that gay people's lives could be as boring as anyone else's, if not more so. Her fans couldn't get enough of her.

All this content distinguished *GCN* from the few other gay publications at the time, which focused on happenings at bars that could be illustrated with photographs of sexy guys and puff pieces about celebrities and local heroes.

GCN's mission was explicitly activist—we wanted to encourage readers to come out of the closet and become involved in the movement and also to provide a forum where ideas and actions could be proposed and debated. We often claimed that *GCN* was neutral, and that we were open to all perspectives, including conservative ones, but that was ridiculous. We supported the most radical expressions of the gay liberation movement. We believed in upsetting the social order and in creating alternatives to traditional gender roles, definitions of sexuality, and hierarchical power structures of all kinds.

The paper never had a circulation of more than five thousand—although at its peak it claimed subscribers in all fifty states and twelve foreign countries. It was always short of money. Our politics frightened off most advertisers. Still, *GCN* had an influence way out of proportion to its circulation figures. I can't count the number of people who have told me that buying a copy was their first step toward coming out, their first inkling that a gay life could be whole and satisfying and could include friendship, community, and love.

GCN was a genuine community effort. The small, ever-changing paid staff and a large, dedicated group of volunteers did everything from writing the articles to laying out the paper to stuffing it into envelopes and sorting it for the post office. Before computers, fax machines, cell phones, or Federal Express, *GCN* appeared every week—including after the 1982 arson fire that destroyed the paper's Bromfield Street office and throughout the crushing, daily crisis of AIDS. (In all its history, *GCN* failed to publish only once, and that wasn't because of the fire but because of the blizzard of 1978. A few staff people clomped through the snow to the office, but with no electricity they could use only the manual typewriters. The room was cold and dark. The phones were down. The typesetter and the printer and the post office were closed, along with just about everything else in eastern Massachusetts, by order of Governor Dukakis. Finally, they locked up and went home.)

Unusual among gay organizations, the *GCN* collective included both women and men from the very beginning and was mixed in terms of class and age. Although many of us were in our twenties, our writers and volunteers included people from their thirties up to their sixties. More typically, it was less diverse in terms of race—most of us were white, although the group also included African Americans, Asians, and Latino/as. The paper rarely shied away from controversial issues; we sought them out and probably even created a few. Reporters, readers, and avid letter-writers brought incredible passion to a wide range of topics: the role of bars in the queer community (which immediately lost *GCN* its most potentially lucrative source of advertising), intergenerational sex, S&M, pornography, drag, racism, sexism, socialism, feminism, reproductive rights, nonmonogamy, U.S. policy in Central America, Democratic and Republican politics—and later, of course, AIDS. The scope of *GCN*'s coverage was itself a source of constant debate: What exactly *was* "gay community news"?

A stint at *GCN* left no one unmarked. We were always on deadline, but we were not simply a newspaper. Ours was the only listing under *gay* in the Boston telephone book; thus, phone duty could involve anything from taking down the copy for a personal ad to giving directions to the gay cruising area in the Fenway Victory Gardens, providing the number of a sympathetic lawyer, or persuading a distraught kid to call the gay youth group instead of committing suicide. The small staff was paid so little to do so much that hardly anyone could tolerate it for very long. Instead, innumerable people, many of whom went on to become leaders of gay and social justice organizations, journalists, authors, and teachers, whirled briefly in and out. *GCN* trained an entire generation of activists. I worked there full time from October 1978 until June 1982 and then volunteered as a board member and writer until I left Boston to go to graduate school in 1985—an eternity in *GCN* years.

The word *homophobia* implies an active fear and hatred, but the situation of lesbians and gay men in the late seventies was somehow even more bizarre: we simply did not exist, especially as far as the media were concerned. One *GCN* news editor used to complain that when he identified himself to sources on the phone, they would say, "You're from where? The *Day* Community News? The *Bay* Community News?" They literally could not hear the word *gay*.

Nevertheless, *Gay Community News* had a palpable effect in the world that was both exhilarating and scary. Demonstrations were organized out of our office; political campaigns launched; romances both fleeting and life-long kindled. We were suing the Federal Bureau of Prisons, and Boston's police union was threatening to sue us. Bullet holes pocked our front windows. Our office was periodically broken into and sacked. But even worse than the mayhem and vandalism were the violence and death. Our people were gay-bashed, thrown out of their homes, fired, committed to mental institutions, murdered. Some killed themselves. Then came AIDS.

Conventional wisdom has it that gay men and lesbians lived and organized politically quite separately from one another, until the AIDS crisis drew us together. Women are marginal in the world portrayed by gay male writers like Edmund White or Andrew Holleran. And many lesbians, influenced by the separatist philosophy of the seventies, paint the mixed gay and lesbian movement as a regressive force. But at *GCN* we took pride in the way men and women had worked together on our paper from its earliest days. As we became not just political colleagues but also dear friends, we created a new ethos, which, through the paper, spread from Boston to the national movement.

I'd known maybe three gay men in my entire life before coming to *GCN*, and when I took the job, fresh from college women's studies courses and volunteering at *Sister Courage*, the local socialist-feminist journal, I thought I would be bringing feminism to the unenlightened—but the men and women at *GCN* were way ahead of me. Instead, I went native. After only a few months and a crash course in gay liberation, I was on the way to developing some of the most profound relationships of my life. If we lesbians and gay men were able to care for one another and struggle together against AIDS, it was because groups like *GCN* sowed the seeds of unity. We now have equal rights laws, Massachusetts marriage licenses, and high school gay/straight alliances, not to mention such unintended consequences as *Queer Eye for the Straight Guy* and *The L Word*, because of the courage and integrity of those early activists, who created a world-changing movement in the face of indifference, hostility, and scorn.

GCN ceased weekly publication in 1992, when changing times worsened its chronic financial problems into a full-blown crisis, and volunteers, subscribers, and advertisers leaked away, but it continued to function as a quarterly and finally as a web publication until finally closing its doors in 1999.

1

The Mystical Hiring Committee of Life

Richard and I used to say we'd have to write the book about *Gay Community News*, before anyone else did it and got it all wrong. But it was clear to me even then that Richard would never write a book. He barely read books, preferring to lug around a week's worth of the *New York Times* in his knapsack until he'd finished every word in every copy, except, naturally, the sports—and a couple of times I caught him glancing at that too. Which just proved it was the comfort of habit and not the content of the *Times*—he genially agreed it was right-wing twaddle—that kept him at it.

Actually, it's hard to imagine how Richard and I thought we could write a book together when we disagreed so much. We debated for years, literally from dawn to dusk, as we worked together at the *GCN* office, went out afterwards for dinner to the whole-wheat pizza place on Charles Street— where you could bring your own jug of red wine and where I more than once pretended I didn't see a little gray mouse leap across the floor and disappear behind the baseboard—and called each other on the phone as soon as we got home.

It's a curious thing about Richard: in any particular group, he's always perceived as the voice of the establishment. This has nothing to do with what he actually says. Maybe it's his height—six feet five. Or his booming voice. Some people are surprised when he tells them he sings bass, like they expect all gay men to be countertenors. Richard used to sing in the choir at Memorial Church in Harvard Yard, and every year we'd have a major argument about his Christmas concert, which he insisted I attend even though he knew I was fed up with Christmas, probably because of my experience in elementary school, where it dominated the entire curriculum from September until winter vacation. The rabbi would tell us little Jews, "Don't you sing those Christmas carols!" while my mother's philosophy was, "You're a child, you like to sing, enjoy yourself." My solution was to sing everything except the references to you-know-who: "Joy to the world/*hmm-hmm* has come." The minister at Richard's Christmas concert was a wonderful old fag who could pronounce the word *Mary* with three or even, if he got particularly carried away, four syllables during the scripture reading, and afterward we were all invited to his lovely home for some holiday cheer. He would greet Richard and me with particular warmth—"Merry Christmas to you and your tribe"—even though at one party, overstimulated by the concert, the eggnog, the obnoxious blinking lights and the cold but jolly pedestrians and their packages jamming Harvard Square, I had such a loud dispute with Richard about that morning's staff meeting that the other guests fled the living room. Richard freshened our drinks, and we settled into the armchairs in front of the roaring fireplace, which we had gotten all to ourselves.

"Your homosexuality *saved* you," I used to tell him. I meant from becoming the corporate lawyer his father wanted him to be, from settling down in the suburbs, from voting Republican, from drinking martinis, from a stifling oppressive middle-class existence. In those days Richard adored Christmas and weddings and graduations and birthday parties, any sort of elaborate social ritual where you got together with your family and smiled until your cheeks got twitchy and your jaw clenched—he absolutely refused to understand why a person might not want to go. He's changed about this, and so have I; these days I'm the one who's always running off to the seder or my parents' anniversary party, convinced they'll love my homosexual self *this time*, while Richard tactfully makes his excuses.

I met Richard Burns in the fall of 1978, when I called the *Gay Community News* office to inquire about the features editor job they were advertising. Richard picked up the phone, and we immediately got into a fight. Explaining the sixty-dollar-a-week salary, Richard said, "It's hard to get used to being poor."

"No one gets *used* to being poor!" I corrected him.

He laughed, "I guess not, doll," and signed me up for an interview. He loved calling everyone *doll*, which he'd picked up from Gregg (La

Principessa) Howe and Harry (Clara) Seng, the ad manager and managing editor, respectively, when Richard had first started working at the
paper. They were Fort Hill Faggots for Freedom, living with about twenty other gay men in several frighteningly dilapidated houses in Roxbury,
unappreciated by the African American neighbors they had so wanted to
cultivate, who were already unhappy about the white Rasta commune that
had moved in down the street. The Faggots ran in and out of one another's
houses, half-naked or wearing dresses. They were notorious, actually, for
wearing dresses, because of an incident in which they had worn them to
invade Sporters, a seedy gay bar on Beacon Hill with boarded-up windows and no sign—I never understood how anyone knew it was called
Sporters. The Faggots and the *GCN* crowd and a number of hustlers and
old men liked to hang out there, and the Faggots decided to protest what
they believed was the bar's insufficient welcome to women. And even
though the serious political point of this *attentat*—as Emma Goldman,
whose autobiography I was reading, would have called it—this zap, was
no doubt obscure to the regulars, it must have worked, because later, when
I was taken there, gathered up by a bunch of volunteers after *GCN* layout
one Thursday night, everyone was perfectly charming to me, waving away
the bills I pulled from my pocket to pay for my beer and inviting me to
dance.

Richard had moved to Boston right after graduating from his snooty
men's college, where he had been the only gay man for miles and miles—
imagine him in all his unmistakable height shining like a beacon as he
walks across the campus. He'd gone directly to *GCN*, where the men said
"doll," and "my dear," and shamelessly waved their arms around, and had
wild sex with each other without a thought of pretending that they were
too drunk to know what they were doing. I picked it all up from Richard—
the mannerisms, not so much the wild sex—once I started working at the
paper.

First, though, I had to be interviewed. By the time I arrived, the *GCN*
interview process had changed. No longer did the entire collective of staff,
volunteers, board members, and hangers-on gather to interrogate potential editors about their views on drag, feminism, semicolons, the inter-
section of race, gender, and the American system of social and economic
class, the nuclear family, intergenerational sex, and the *GCN* advertising policy, which strictly forbade publishing ads that exploited the human

body to sell things, although what constituted exploitation was a matter of perpetual debate. (Why *couldn't* a gay bar depict a humpy sailor, for example, when the customers' hopes of meeting such a person were exactly the point? On the other hand, the odds of their actually encountering a sailor were not good.) Instead, I was interviewed by a committee, a step away from pure democracy that some condemned as elitist but that was less likely to scare away the few applicants willing to attempt subsistence on a *GCN* salary.

As it turned out, that hiring committee was not simply interviewing me for a job. It was nothing less than the mystical hiring committee for the rest of my life. Richard and Harry were on it. And Roberta Stone, although she and I wouldn't get together for another ten years. (To be honest, I don't exactly remember Roberta on the committee, but she insisted again this morning over breakfast that she absolutely was, so I am putting her in.) And Eric Rofes, the outgoing features editor, who tried to be a sort of mentor to me—although when I took his advice and headlined the review of a book about male nudes in art "Cheesecake through the Ages," it infuriated the reviewer, an art history professor who said it was trivializing and anyway should have been *beefcake*, a usage I had to admit I'd never heard before, thus totally embarrassing myself. Sometimes in the middle of the night I still wonder: What if they'd rejected me at that crucial moment? Where would I be now?

It's not a complete exaggeration to say that I was awestruck by my first experience of the *GCN* office. From the street you climbed a steep flight of stairs and entered through the open door on your left, and there you were, right in the middle of it. It was like any newspaper office, in a way— toppling piles of back issues, magazines, papers, notepads, and strange hardcover books that no one would ever review much less read, banks of dented file cabinets, telephones ringing, typewriters chattering and dinging, staffers muttering and grumbling, a refrigerator full of half-eaten sandwiches and cans of Coke. But then there were the bullet holes in the front windows. And behind the long light tables of the art department in the back of the room, separated from the *GCN* office by a partition, the office of *FagRag*, an anarchist collective vaguely contiguous with the Fort Hill Faggots. At unpredictable intervals they would publish a journal that had somehow come to the attention of William Loeb, the infamously conservative publisher of the Manchester, New Hampshire, *Union Leader*,

FagRagger Charley Shively, wearing his Harvard robe, prepares to burn a Bible during his 1977 gay pride speech. Photo by Ken Rabb.

who had termed it "the most loathsome publication in the English language"—a motto the FagRaggers gleefully pasted all over their masthead. The year they unfurled a gay pride banner that read, in black letters on pink taffeta, PORNOGRAPHY, PROSTITUTION, PROMISCUITY, PEDERASTY! their slogan so dismayed a large contingent of the *GCN* membership that a vote to terminate their sublease nearly succeeded—although it's not clear how this rule would have been enforced, since the FagRaggers had already vigorously demonstrated their scorn for legal documents such as subleases. During his speech at the 1977 gay pride march, FagRagger Charley Shively had incinerated not only Leviticus 20:13 ("If a man also lie with mankind, as he lieth with a woman, both of them have committed an abomination: they shall surely be put to death"), but also a stack of other symbolic documents—his Harvard Ph.D., his insurance policies, a dollar bill, and the Massachusetts Criminal Code, Chapter 272, section 35 ("Unnatural and Lascivious Acts")—though the Bible is the only thing most people remember. As he touched match to paper, audience members began shouting: "Burn it! Burn it!" and "No, no, not the Bible!" I'm sure the incident headlines right-wing fundraising letters to this day—"Homosexuals Burn the Holy Book!"

What really got to me, though, were the newspapers on the walls. The covers of every issue *GCN* had ever published were displayed in rows starting at the ceiling and extending around the entire perimeter of the room. Who knows whose idea it had originally been? It probably just happened, the sudden inspiration of a volunteer with a staple gun. The cumulative effect was impressive. Once I started working at the paper, I would feel newly inspired each morning when I glanced around the office and saw all that we had accomplished over the years. That is, when I didn't feel completely disheartened. Photos and drawings were expensive, and budget aside, it was just hard to come up with a striking, relevant cover week after week. So covers were the sites of some of our worst mistakes: ugly, trivial, obnoxious. At staff meetings we regularly had terrible arguments about the cover, except when the art director succeeded in keeping it under wraps until Thursday night layout, when it was too late to change it. I doubt we ever published a cover that anyone was completely satisfied with, although of course we sometimes claimed to be, depending on the position we'd taken in the week's debate. And there they all were, staring us in the face.

Maybe it was the cover display that gave rise to the practice of sticking anything whatever on the walls. Everyone who entered the office eventually participated in the unintentional, collective creation of the collage of clippings, doodles, quotes, snapshots, to-do lists, postcards, cartoons, hate mail, love letters, long-lost telephone numbers, political leaflets, placards from demonstrations, photos from magazines gay and straight of buff guys in various postures, all without shirts, and an Elaine-Noble-for-State-Representative styrofoam boater hat with red, white, and blue band. Things were constantly being added, and no one ever bothered to take anything down, so that at eye level, below the orderly rows of covers, was a chaos of layers upon layers of an ever-evolving Artwork of the People.

The trick question at my interview was about the picture on the latest *FagRag* cover. Just, you know, did I like it? The FagRaggers had submitted it as the illustration for an exchange ad they were placing in *GCN* and must have been at that very moment reveling in the predictable uproar among their landlords about whether the image was beautiful, vulgar, exploitative, oppressive to women, or a proud expression of gay male sexuality. I had some trouble making it out at first—and no, it was not my lesbian lack of familiarity, thank you. It's some sort of figure/ground perceptual problem: I can't see the bat in the Batman logo either. Eventually I made out a pen-and-ink drawing of a large, flaccid penis surrounded by a lot of confusing hair and excited brush strokes. Simultaneously I realized that the committee members ranged before me represented the various positions in the debate about it, and although I knew nothing about *FagRag* or their lease or the staff's weekly acrimonious debates about covers and ads, I sensed that anything I said to please one faction would inevitably alienate the rest.

"It wouldn't sell me a magazine," I offered brightly.

This answer was apparently equivocal enough to appease most of the committee, and by the time I left we were all feeling so pleased with one another that when I got back to my apartment my phone was already ringing. It was Richard offering me the job.

"I have to think about it," I said, mostly because I had a vague idea that it was more professional to make a show of playing hard to get. "Can I call you back tomorrow morning?"

"What for?" said Richard. "Just say yes now. You know you want to."

As in so many things from that day to this, he was right.

"You'll love us," he said. "You'll see."

I was ambivalent about becoming friends with Richard. I wasn't sure what I, as a lesbian, thought, or should think, about men; nor about what I imagined was the power inherent in our positions as editors of a national gay newspaper. But he persisted in inviting me to dinner. Finally I accepted, but showed up two hours late, because I had gotten a last-minute urge to work alongside the Friday Folders, the *GCN* proletariat, so to speak—the volunteers who stuffed the newspapers into plain brown envelopes every week, because if we'd mailed the paper to people's homes with the word *gay* on the cover in all its glory, we would have had even fewer subscribers. Once, we received a series of phone calls from a furious reader—all of our readers called us, we knew practically every one of them personally—during which he shrieked that he was going to have to sell his house and move to parts unknown, because his flap had come unstuck. He was sure his neighbors or at least his mailman had peeked in and learned his secret.

The volunteers were called the Friday Folders because the original *GCN* mailing routine had involved first folding the papers in half and then stuffing them into six-by-nine envelopes, until some circulation manager had the brilliant idea of ordering nine-by-twelves, thereby eliminating the folding step, although not its alliterative allure. The most improbable combinations of people would turn up, dyke separatists and A-list gay politicos, all looking for something useful to do on a slow weekend, or for a new friend and some free pizza and beer.

Richard loved inviting people to dinner. It was too bad he couldn't cook. That eventually became my job. We'd run out to the particularly nasty A&P near his house—the produce was prehistoric—where he'd insist on scrutinizing the ingredients and assessing the price per pound of every item before allowing me to put it in the cart, like suddenly he was Betty Crocker. Dinner had to be a dish that didn't require a lot of spices or pots, because he didn't keep many supplies on hand beyond what I'd bought the last time, except the ingredients for Chicken Divan, his one specialty—chicken breasts, broccoli, a can of mushroom soup *and* a can of celery soup, grated cheese. It was out of this world, I don't know why he never makes it anymore.

But he must have truly wanted to impress me that first night, because he cooked not Chicken Divan but steak—Italian style, with a little Ragu tomato sauce on top. Luckily, I'm not a vegetarian, not even a *fowl vegetarian*, as Eric once characterized himself. Richard said nothing about my lateness, but poured me a glass of red wine, and we sat down at the table and spent the rest of the evening yelling and interrupting each other and waving our arms around, Richard refilling my glass, until nearly midnight. The last train from the South End, where he lived, to my neighborhood in Cambridge would leave at any minute. Richard leapt up when I did, and we threw on our coats and breathlessly sprinted the two blocks to the old Dover Street station, Richard chanting "Go, Aim, go!" when I faltered—he had the advantage in leg length—and practically pushing me up the two flights of stairs to the elevated tracks. He somehow gave me a quick hug and simultaneously a final shove through the door of the last car. Laughing and gasping for breath I slid down the long slippery bench as the doors closed and the train pulled out of the station, and I dimly saw Richard waving at me—goodbye, goodbye—through the scratched window.

Once that first dinner broke the ice, Richard and I became constant companions—work, dinner, movies, meetings, brunch. Sunday mornings he would sing in the choir and then run off from church to check out the action in the Harvard Science Center men's room, pick up a *Times* in the Square, and show up at my house, ready for coffee and bagels. And when I had dinner at his apartment, rather than worry about catching the train, I often slept over on the couch in his living room. It was dark red leather, the kind of thing that must have come from his father's study, and long enough for me or even Richard to stretch out on. The pillows were soft and deep and should have given me a terrible backache, but I'd sink into them and pull Richard's sleeping bag over my head. (This was the same notorious sleeping bag from which, a few years later, both Urvashi Vaid and I caught crabs, even though she and I had broken up at that point. We'd slept at Richard's on successive nights, and he'd claimed he was cured and the sleeping bag was nit-free. I was so horrified to find such things infesting my person—and to have to point them out to the kindly lesbian doctor at the gay health clinic—that I not only washed myself and my hair many times over with the special carcinogenic soap she pre-scribed but also laundered all my clothing and every piece of fabric in my apartment, including the curtains.) In those days I lived alone, and I wouldn't have changed that—I'd proven too many times my terrible judg-ment when it came to choosing roommates whose dogs ran away when-ever you cracked open the front door, or who thought you could concoct a tasty dinner by combining all the leftovers in the refrigerator into one big casserole, or who left it to me to haul all the recycling out each week because they knew I wished to live lightly upon the earth. But it lifted my habitual insomnia to know Richard was out there somewhere, puttering around his darkened rooms.

In the mornings I would invent errands to do on the way to the office so we wouldn't arrive together, because who knows what everyone would have made of that, and I didn't want to provide encouragement for the rumors of conspiracy that accrued around practically anything. The truth is, arguing aside, from the moment I was hired Richard and I were always seen, correctly after all, as a bloc. The mystical committee, with unerring karmic instinct, had found me my niche.

BIPAD: 65498

ISSN: 0147-0728

VOL. 7, NO. 26

THE GAY WEEKLY 50¢

JANUARY 26, 1980

GayCommunityNews

**Californians
March on
Sacramento**

**International
Gay
Association**

**Anti-Lesbian
Film Opens
in N.Y.C.**

An American Lesbian in Paris

2

My Yale College and My Harvard

"A whale-ship was my Yale College and my Harvard," says Ishmael, in a book some will tell you is by a gay author, and you can almost believe them, remembering that insanely over-the-top last scene, the *Pequod* sucked down into the deep and Ahab flailing about on the back of the furious leviathan, which he will ride forever and ever across the seven seas, for god's sake. Or maybe that was just Gregory Peck. But there's still all that stuff about how Ish ends up sleeping with Queequeg in *New Bedford*—get it?—and Queequeg's glorious skill with a harpoon. I read *Moby Dick* in high school, and I'm one of those people who didn't skip the whaling chapters, because I loved every minute of that book, the exoticism and yet dailiness of life aboard ship, the small clan isolated in the great sea pursuing a mad ideal.

My whale-ship was *GCN*, even though unlike Ishmael I had the advantage of college, two of them in fact, since I dropped out of the first. But college wasn't for me, and I at one time I even felt sorry for people who said it was the best time of their lives—although lately I've come to envy those non-alienated souls a bit, the ones whose roommates became their lifelong friends, who adored their courses, were invited to dinner with their professors, studied in Paris for a semester, and graduated with honors while their proud parents snapped pictures. I might have liked studying in Paris.

But that's not my story. I wasn't interested in any of that, then. I was looking for the Movement. I had protested against the Vietnam War while I was in high school. I used to hand out leaflets in front of the building before the first bell rang—always making sure to give one to my home-room teacher, who would then mark me late, although she knew perfectly well that I was present on school grounds, as the rules required. And I marched in some of the larger, more peaceful demonstrations: once I rode a bus to Washington and slept on a church pew, and another time I went with my mother, pushing my youngest brother in a stroller. At a Ruther-ford, New Jersey, city council meeting I had stood up and declared that I was ready to "aid and abet draft resisters," which I understood to be some kind of illegal formula. I was waiting for the FBI to ring the doorbell, but the only person who ever showed up was a classmate's angry father, look-ing not for me but for my younger sister Judy, who had founded an under-ground newspaper that included the address of Planned Parenthood, and distributed it around the ninth grade. My father, who has always enjoyed a good debate, invited the man in for coffee.

Only a few of the geekiest students joined me in my antiwar actions, and I wasn't looking for those kinds of student protesters, the ones like me. I longed to find the ones I'd read about in the newspaper, who were creating a new world by staying up all night debating philosophy and politics, by growing their hair long and wearing miniskirts, by expanding their minds and making love not war. I believed that when I got to college my days of wandering alone or with my mother in the crowd would be over. I would find my proper contingent. So college was a horrible disap-pointment, probably the biggest letdown of my life—and that includes my first, ten-minute experience of sexual intercourse. Most of the people I met could have gone to my high school. A few of them *had* gone to my high school, and from there, like me, to Douglass, New Jersey's college for women.

This was a school that had included in its list of items the incoming first-year student should bring with her *one pair of white gloves.* They were to be worn to shake the hand of the college president at the welcoming tea we would attend during our first semester. What kind of person—in 1970! Only weeks after the bombing of Cambodia and the murders at Kent State!—had gloves? I had no intention of acquiring them. When the time came, I was duly invited, only to become overwhelmed with anxiety about how I'd be treated if I turned up barehanded. Beyond that, I told myself, what did I know of this president? She could be a warmonger, a defender of the establishment, an enforcer of parietal hours and in loco parentis. Not the kind of person with whom I should break bread. Some of the other new girls in my dorm, oblivious to the glove and political issues, went to the party. It was okay, they said. The president seemed nice. What do you mean, gloves? This has always been my problem: rebellious, questioning—but reluctant to do anything that might make anyone uncomfortable or cause a scene. Black gloves, elbow length, did not occur to me. As a women's college, the school had all kinds of little traditions and rituals, and the president's tea was only the first from which I opted out.

Which might have been a mistake. White gloves excepted, the nature of the college rituals, the whole meaning of a women's college, was changing. In my dorm, the senior-class house chair*man*, as she was titled, was an old-style Douglass student, who wore a college blazer, probably owned drawersful of white gloves, and was engaged to a Rutgers Deke. Yet, at the same time, women's studies classes were proliferating, and the new generation of student leaders were a bunch of women whom I found wildly intriguing, who dressed in overalls and eventually revealed themselves to be a coven of pothead dyke goddess-worshipers. I first encountered them at orientation, which they had volunteered to organize. They had hired a hot-air balloon, which unfortunately never got off the ground, to give the new students an unusual perspective on the campus. In a more successful session, a ceramics major taught the craft of controlling the forces generated by the whirling of the pottery wheel to center and mold a lump of clay—a lesson that, it was hoped, we would find relevant during our first year on our own. At the winter solstice, a line of students danced through the campus on the cold, dark evening, holding candles and chanting. The college emblem, the Douglass fir, took on druidical significance.

Early in my junior year, the poet Adrienne Rich, who had recently come out as a lesbian, visited our campus. She read from her new book, *Diving into the Wreck*. My attention momentarily caught, I heard her intone, ". . . the wreck and not the story of the wreck / The thing itself and not the myth." *The thing itself and not the myth.* Yes! Boom! Right there in the glaring fluorescence and uncomfortable little desks of an English department classroom, I had an epiphany, exactly as defined by my professor and described by James Joyce in *Portrait of the Artist*. It all came together: my inability to find a focus for my studies, or soul-mates among the girls in my dormitory, or political comrades. It was time for me to go out into the world. I'd read up on Joyce's formula: silence, exile, cunning.

The dean was not sympathetic when I explained why I needed a leave of absence. "Maybe people like you do not belong in college," she said.

People like me—meaning people who changed their majors more than four times in two years? Incipient lesbians? Political radicals? I never found out exactly what she had in mind, but since she refused my request for a leave, I dropped out altogether and followed my boyfriend and my best friend, both of whom I wished were a little more interested in me sexually, to Boston.

I didn't completely cut my ties to Douglass. One memorable weekend I returned for a concert by Lavender Jane, three lesbian folksingers who refused to perform if men were in the audience. The inevitable guy-asserting-his-right-to-free-assembly tried to crash the gate. After lengthy whispered negotiations among the singers, the concert producers, and the student body president, who happened to be in attendance and was afraid she would be held personally liable for any Bill of Rights violations, Lavender Jane suggested we close down the concert as a public event. The audience began filing quietly out of the hall, and then at a signal from Lavender Jane, the student body president weeping beside them onstage, we turned around and burst back in again, harmonizing to LJ's best-known lyric,

> Any woman can
> be a lezz-bee-ann.

We reconvened as an invitation-only, private meeting. It was a heady moment, but essentially extracurricular. I occasionally considered returning to school at Douglass, but despite Lavender Jane and women's studies, I was finding a lot more happening in the outside world, specifically, Cambridge, Massachusetts, 1973.

People talk about the sixties, but it was the seventies when the world really seemed like it was about to change forever. Maybe that's why the decade has such a bad reputation. On TV, it's all flowered shirts with funny collars and bell-bottom pants and disco—not that there's anything wrong with disco. At *Gay Community News* we analyzed the "I hate disco" movement among college boys as nothing less than homophobic code for "I hate *fags*"—the way Nixon said *New York* on the tapes when he really meant *Jew*. The seventies need rehabilitation. The war was ending, the long dark years of atrocity and protest. War criminals Nixon and Kissinger were out of power. Rising up, it seemed to me, were the voices of women, of black people, of Chicanos, of youth and elders in a beautiful chorus.

Or does everyone feel that way at twenty-two? On the one hand, parties, meetings, demonstrations, poetry. On the other hand, confusion and misery. My boyfriend and I broke up, and I developed a series of long, hopeless obsessions with one woman after another: Marty, my best friend, who came out but then stopped speaking to me, because she was a separatist and didn't consider me a lesbian, since she had rejected my advances and I hadn't yet been successful with anyone else; Tracy, my co-worker one summer, who was herself also obsessed although unfortunately for me with African men, whom she picked up at the various university libraries around town; Jenny, my intriguing new downstairs neighbor. I was having no sex and few dates, which was not only depressing but also humiliating—weren't my twenties were supposed to be the most sexy, fun years of my life? Instead I was isolated, with no idea how I would ever cross the apparently insurmountable barrier from no-touch to touch.

Although I hadn't developed much more of an academic sense of purpose than I had when I quit Douglass, I decided to finish college. My parents had been saving for my tuition since I was two years old. I realized that I would never be able move on to anything else in life until I graduated, even though part of me condemned my desire for a college degree as hopelessly bourgeois. I enrolled at Brandeis as a commuting transfer student, an anomaly on a campus where nearly everyone else lived in the dorms or occasionally down the hill in Waltham, an impoverished industrial town that in its heyday had been known for the manufacture of reliable watches. I arranged to get rides to campus from a graduate student couple in Cambridge, who used the commute to catch up on the arguing they hadn't had time to do at home because they'd been busy writing their dissertations. When that got too uncomfortable, I would take the train. The conductors would announce the Brandeis stop, Roberts Street, as the brakes screeched and bells clanged, yelling over the noise in their townie accents, "Rrr-abbits, Rrr-abbits." I traveled to my classes as if to a job, barely speaking to anyone while I was there, although I did get involved in a student strike during which we took over the sociology building. We had nothing against the sociologists, who were among our staunchest supporters, but attempting to occupy the Brandeis student center was well known to be a doomed strategy. According to rumor, the center had been built in the glory days of student radicalism at the school, when professors like Herbert Marcuse taught students like Angela Davis, and it was specifically designed to be ugly, uncomfortable, and above all impregnable, with entrances and exits on many levels and corridors snaking every which way. I still have nightmares that I am lost among them. Certainly I was never able to find my way around the building, or to locate the commuter lounge that it supposedly housed.

What's remarkable to me now is how little sense of possibility I had, especially for a child of the middle class. I didn't see college as something that would set me on the path to the rest of my life; instead, it felt more like a detour. At Brandeis, I settled down to a major in English, although I saw this choice as something of a defeat, since I had previously reasoned that I read books all the time, and if my parents were going to spend all that money on my college education the least I could do was to study something I couldn't learn on my own, such as experimental psychology or music theory. I played the violin with enthusiasm and diligence but little talent, and abandoned that particular major after a conference with the department chair, a maniacal cellist, who leaned across his desk, his eyes glittering, and said, "So, will you give us a rip-roaring senior recital?" Since the greatest compliment my teacher, Mr. Kovacs, a depressive elderly Hungarian, ever dispensed was, "Zis vas qvite *decent*, Emmy"—I had to admit that I probably would not.

I had little hope that the guidance and insights of a teacher would enhance my reading experiences, but I knew that an English major was something I could at least complete. Secretly I wanted to be a writer. Boys in my English seminars would occasionally declare themselves to be writers between puffs on their pipes—students then were allowed to smoke in class—and their audacity almost made me faint.

The only other careers that had ever truly interested me were teacher and book editor, but by the time I finished high school the idea of having to amuse a classroom full of adolescents for hours on end was terrifying. And I had no idea how one went about becoming a book editor. Jenny, my intriguing downstairs neighbor, explained to me that she planned eventually to be promoted from her assistant job to an editorial position; the company she worked for did not publish the novels that I loved to read, though, but magazines with titles like *Packaging Digest* and *Material*

Handling Product News. I had no problem with doing menial office work, but her experience did not look promising in terms of getting on a track to something more interesting, and in any case this sort of career planning implied a level of worldly ambition that I scorned. I couldn't see working my way up to a position at the top of the masthead of, say, *Food Engineering & Ingredients.* Actually I should have hit Jenny up for a complimentary subscription to *FE & I,* which was just the kind of thing my father, a salesman for a manufacturer of food colorings and flavorings, would have found fascinating and useful. My parents' coffee table was piled high with exactly those kinds of amazingly boring magazines.

I didn't want to be like my parents, whose first purchase when they set up housekeeping together had been a stove. I immediately spent whatever money they gave me on books and record albums and movie tickets and violin lessons. I assumed I would never qualify for a paying job that was fulfilling and socially useful. Instead I envisioned myself working in a succession of dead-end positions and discovering my life's meaning in my political work, the poems and stories I wrote on scraps of paper and showed to no one, and the G-major scale in thirds and octaves, which I would someday learn to play perfectly in tune.

3

Cynthia, Goddess of the Moon

Virginia Woolf, or Virginia Stephen as she was then, and her sister Vanessa were touring the Louvre when they spied an entourage that included one of their Stephen aunts, and Virginia jumped behind a pillar to hide. The incident exemplified something for Virginia—the sisters' youthful determination to evade the Victorian tastes and *moeurs* of their distinguished family; the futility of escape, as she was inevitably discovered in her absurd hideout. She referred to it comically in her journals and letters, which I read as they were published one by one during the 1970s, by which time most of the people who would have been offended by Virginia's wicked tongue and unfair, even lunatic, judgments had died. I loved Virginia—not for her suicide, I wasn't that kind of adolescent—but for her wit, her talent, her imagery and style, her beauty, her enviable circle. I agreed with whoever it was who said that her greatest achievement, even more than the novels or the criticism, was the journals. After their publication, what circle of gay friends with intellectual and artistic pretensions did not imagine itself the new Bloomsbury? The social whirl, the outrageous pranks, the polymorphous sexual melodrama, the lives successfully dedicated to literature and art. And yet Virginia trembles behind her pillar, terrified of meeting Auntie.

The countless pillars I've hidden behind.

Finally it's become a reflex, a bad, awful habit. I see someone I know in the supermarket, on the street, or let's say on the subway, and I raise my newspaper before my face, engrossed. Or I simply pretend I'm someone else. My face isn't that distinctive—so it's quite possible, isn't it, that I'm not who you thought I was, but am in fact staring with the implacable gaze of a stranger right through you?

I can't rationalize this behavior by pretending I do it to avoid people I don't like, although sometimes that's certainly the case. But more often it's someone I like perfectly well, or even very much, or worst of all, whom I admire. For example, Michelle Baxter—tall, beautiful, dreadlocked, absolutely the coolest person I know, and amazingly enough, always perfectly kind and friendly to me. Yet I've ignored her sitting across from me in the subway car. I've pretended to read the newspaper, all the while in a paralytic panic that she's seen me and has concluded that I'm some kind of weird racist. The next time I see her I resolve to say hello—I do it—she hugs me. Yes, I've been hugged on the subway for all to see by the glamorous Michelle Baxter. Why then do I avoid her the next time?

I make these kinds of resolutions constantly, to greet friend and stranger alike in a friendly and forthright manner. I used to practice in the elevator at work at one of my early jobs. The elevator terrified me at first, not because I was phobic about the contraption itself but because of the chatting required on the ride. The *Boston Globe* has reported the discovery of a shyness gene. My mother claims I cried at the sight of strangers even as an infant—mostly at the sight of men, actually, after I'd met the pediatrician with his black bag full of needles and his habit of pinching babies' cheeks, hard. Oh the pain of living in a world jammed with people who jostle, poke, and shout.

All this is to say that I can't explain how I ended up in bed with my first girlfriend. Think of me at that electrifying moment—her hand on my breast, her breath in my ear. Me, I don't dare breathe, because I'm suddenly poised at the brink of the inevitable, it's happening, right here, right now. My life is changing.

I have no memory of that moment whatsoever. It's unfair, the way some things stay with you and some don't. My memory is exactly like my totally boring journals—stuffed with ephemera, anxious speculation, and imagined slights. Yet where are those times I might actually enjoy revisiting? *Ou sont les neiges d'antan?* as we learned to demand in French class: *Where are the snows of yesteryear?* Melted, naturally, and drained away.

Desire must finally have trumped shyness. She must have given me an opening, made a move. A small gesture would have been enough. I'd never dared to say anything to any of the women I'd been obsessed with previously, although not because I was afraid of or repulsed by the idea of becoming a lesbian. Not at all! I believed that with the bursting forth of feminism and gay liberation, society was hurtling beyond homophobia. Led—why not?—by lesbians, it would soon take off in a new, revolutionary direction, except maybe in a few unfortunate locations such as Iowa. My problem was rather that I was in awe of these lesbians and convinced none would have me. Even when Jenny asked me right to my face, "Are you in love with me?" I said, "No, no, no"—simultaneously drawing out my denial and horribly regretting my lie—"Not like that."

I was helping her move her living room couch back into place after a party at which it had become clear during the dancing that she and a poet we knew, whom I had also felt drawn to, had crossed the sexual borderline that still remained closed to me. Even as we grappled the couch across the room, Jenny was glowing with the glow of poetry. And thus I believed I'd lost forever the tiny chance I'd had with her, not to mention with the poet, although I barely allowed myself to think of that, since someone who was both a lesbian and a poet seemed so far beyond me.

I have no idea where Jenny is these days, or what she thinks of her old adventures. But I occasionally run into her poet—we've become quite friendly—and over drinks she once asked, "How do I know you, anyway?"

"Once upon a time," I said lightly, "you and my downstairs neighbor, the lovely Jenny . . ."

She looked genuinely baffled. "Who?"

I could not bring myself to remind her of what for me had been the romance and torment of their relationship.

After the poet, Jenny got involved with a novelist, but then decided to become straight and apply to business school. She broke up with her novelist. By that time she and I were no longer neighbors, and she called to ask if I'd spend the night with her, because even though she was the one who'd ended her relationship, she was feeling sad and lonely and in need of some reassurance from her loyal old pal. I threw toothbrush, underwear, and book into my knapsack, strapped on my bicycle helmet, and pedaled madly to her through the nighttime traffic. In bed each of us kept scrupulously to her own side, and in the morning, watching Jenny fasten her bra, I saw that one of her beautiful breasts was bigger than the other. Still I didn't breathe a word about my feelings, although I could see that, decisions aside, Jenny would continue to fall for girls.

The name of my first lesbian lover was Cynthia—like the goddess of the moon. We met in 1976, when we were both writing for *Sister Courage*, Boston's socialist-feminist newspaper. There was another feminist newspaper in town too, *Sojourner*, but it was capitalist—published out of a borrowed office at MIT by an owner who thought she could make a go of it as a business. *Sister Courage* meetings were held around town at volunteers' apartments or at the Cambridge Women's Center, established just a few years before, when a building takeover at Harvard had been resolved by an anonymous donor, who got the protesters out by giving them a falling-down house in Central Square. Unfortunately this generous gift caused the Women's Center collective incalculable agony, since property is theft and owning a building a middle-class privilege. Then again, if they sold it, they'd be stuck with a pile of cash. It was impossible to get rid of the thing cleanly, which must be a lesson of some kind, and of course if they had figured out a way to do it that would have meant the end of the center, and having one had been the whole point, hadn't it? Meanwhile, as most of the women sat on the living room floor debating all this, others—the butchier lesbians—were chasing away the neighborhood thugs and fixing the boiler.

I was living on the third floor of an all-women triple-decker in Somerville across from the train tracks and the Sears. When the landlord came to collect the rent or fix the furnace he teased us about being man-haters, but we put up with it, because when we talked to him we realized he was angry at many of the same inequities we were, he just blamed the completely wrong people, like black people. I was trying to figure out how to redirect him.

It was my first-floor neighbor Suzanne who had invited me to my first *Sister Courage* meeting. When *SC* had its lesbian/straight split—all feminist groups split in those days—Suzanne, Cynthia, and I joined up with the lesbians, although I of course was anxious about whether they'd have me. Cynthia and I were assigned to cover a big women's music festival in Cambridge. Women's music was like folk music only instead of Pete Seeger—who once said a very friendly "Hi" to me on a street corner in Greenwich Village after an Earth Day rally—the performers were these cute lesbians who swapped the pronouns in the old songs to loud cheers from the audience, or wrote their own when necessary. A favorite was "Ode to a Gym Teacher." Was it during the festival weekend that Cynthia first kissed me, sweeping away all the pillars and posts of shyness, and we found our way to bed?

At one point she stopped me saying, "You don't have to do that—it's your first time."

It hadn't occurred to me not to admit to that. "Please," I said. "I've wanted to for so long." Although this wasn't technically true—my fantasies having been ecstatic yet vague—I would have done anything not to disappoint her. And yes, I wanted this, her, now, and had all along without exactly realizing it.

Was I surprised at the taste of her?

Maybe I wasn't surprised at all.

Afterward she fell asleep. I lay awake marveling at my situation. A lesbian—Cynthia!—in my arms. When the sun came shining through the bedroom window and woke her the next morning, she looked at me unhappily. On a whim she had kissed me, and now, she suddenly realized, I was hers—imprinted on her like a fuzzy baby duck, to toddle after her everywhere she went. And it's true, she was ever on my mind; for example, if I bought a spiral notebook or a pair of sneakers, I would think: *Cynthia would never write in a notebook like this*, or *Cynthia will like my feet in these sneakers.*

In her real life, when she wasn't volunteering at *Sister Courage* or going out to lesbian bars, Cynthia was a high-school English teacher in a dismal working-class suburb located at an inconvenient distance from Boston, where the parents all had long, infuriating commutes and even the more sophisticated students were convinced that if they ever set foot downtown they'd instantly be knifed or beheaded or something. When I first met her she had been on sabbatical, and she had just returned from driving cross-country in her VW bug. In every town she came to she hooked up with the lesbians—she found the women's center or the bookstore or tagged along with a demonstration. In Arizona, she camped out in the desert at the Nourishing Space for Women, an enterprise she'd heard about from a Tucson bartender, where a group of lesbians planned to support themselves through tourism and earthworm farming. The head of the Space had shaved off all her hair, and instead of renaming herself Moondyke or Treewomon as so many had done, used a curt monosyllable, Kat or Bree, something like that. She and Cynthia had an affair while Cynthia stuck around and helped her repair the visitors' cabins and do the daily chores like turning over the dirt in the worm-beds.

ARTEMIS PRODUCTIONS PRESENTS:

THE SECOND BOSTON WOMEN'S MUSIC FESTIVAL

SPONSORED BY THE RADCLIFFE WOMEN'S CENTER

APRIL 1·2·3.

Cynthia and I would go on excursions in her VW. I have a photo of her sitting on the beach in Marblehead, laughing. Laughter has thrown her forward into the frame, her hair falling in her face. She holds nothing back. I have another of her at the summit of a Berkshire hill we'd climbed. Her feet are planted on the ground, and she grins as if she discovered the place. But her spirit changed when she went back to teaching. She lived every minute in terror of being exposed. On the morning of the gay pride march—my first, because before Cynthia I hadn't felt qualified to partici-pate—Cynthia, like many of the others in the gay teachers' contingent, disguised herself by putting a Stop & Shop bag over her head. Uncomfort-able, she changed it at the last minute for a flowered pillowcase, which I approved as possibly cooler than brown paper in the June sun. But even in her disguise, she panicked when we arrived at the march, imagining that passersby might recognize her by her hands, swinging ungloved at her sides. She and her roommates had made a sign that said, "Gay Teachers: Proud but Not Free."

As Cynthia turned paranoid, I desired her more than ever. Sometimes my devotion pleased her, but usually she found it annoying. I couldn't make her happy. She was so different from me—working class, blonde, non-Jewish. And she wasn't a modern, liberated type of lesbian, who could carelessly go to the gay pride march or kiss her girlfriend on the street; at her high school she lived in a time-warp of intolerance. Eventually it made her literally sick; she had the flu for weeks, and I took her temperature and cooked chicken soup and ran out to the women's bookstore to buy her a gift—*Twenty-one Love Poems* by Adrienne Rich, my favorite. I aimed to become indispensable.

Movie night at Bread and Roses, the women's restaurant. I take my seat. It's The Children's Hour, *a film I've never seen before: Audrey Hepburn and Shirley MacLaine are teachers accused of perversion. The audience laughs all the way through it, harder and harder as the creepy story unfolds until the end when Shirley admits her desire and hangs herself. "Not that again!" the audience hoots. The movie lesbian's torment seems so pointless and corny, now that we've come out in large numbers and marched and published newspapers and danced at the bar and gathered at the women's restaurant. But I'm crying. Cynthia's getting ready to leave me. She's left me before, but this time I know it will be for good.*

The terrible school year finally came to an end, and Cynthia recovered from her flu and decided to take a vacation. I wasn't invited. "We don't have to do every little thing together," she said. "I should see other friends, too, don't you think?" She was going on a camping trip. I got a postcard. She was sleeping under the stars, the weather was beautiful. In the city it was hot, unrelenting, record-breaking. Then I heard that Cynthia was back in town, but she didn't call me until two days after she returned. She said she would pick me up, and we would go to the air-conditioned movies, but she was parking the car in front of the theater, and she still hadn't kissed me hello. I tried to pull her to me, and she said, "I've fallen in love." She made a speedy U-turn out of the space and kept her eyes on the road all the way back to my apartment. I stole a glance at her while she was driving, and she looked great, all tanned and buff and full of suppressed excitement. She pulled up to my house, and we sat next to each other in the car, and I thought of all the unbearable things Cynthia would have said and done out there in the New Hampshire woods, with nothing between her and her friends and the sky. I got out of the car, and almost before I could slam the door, she pulled away.

Mornings were the worst, waking each day to realize my situation all over again. Cynthia, gone. It was so unfair. I had stuck with her through her bad times, school and sickness, and now that she was feeling better, I'd been tossed aside. I got sick myself for a week with a terrible cold, and Cynthia showed up at my apartment with a guilt-offering of chocolate ice cream, which I guess was nice of her, but I couldn't eat it. I just wanted her to leave.

I had been saving my vacation time at work to go away with Cynthia, but now I used it in an attempt to escape my misery by traveling to the Michigan Womyn's Music Festival with a lesbian I'd met at the office and her girlfriend. I was aware that I didn't really know them well enough for us to be stuck together for a long trip, especially in a car that had only an AM radio, but they had invited me, even knowing I had no license and couldn't help with the driving. They may not have realized that I was also hopeless as a navigator, couldn't tell amusing life stories to entertain the driver on the vampire shift, and would need their help setting up my borrowed tent. The festival had been one of Cynthia's stops on her road trip, and she and others in the *Sister Courage* lesbian caucus had described it glowingly: *five thousand lesbians* (that was the meaning of *womyn*).

Gwen Avery performing at a
women's music festival.
Photo by Susan Fleischmann.

The first night at the festival it rained cats and dogs. Or some kind of small animals. One scurried over the top of my tent, breaking the seal and causing water to pour in. It was already coming up through the floor, since I hadn't known to put down a ground cloth or dig a trench. Lightning strobed all around. I lay in a puddle trying to sleep, as my sleeping bag and clothes got wetter and wetter.

At dawn, the sun broke through as though nothing had happened, and my tent quickly became a steam bath. A woman came by gathering up people's clothes to dry at the laundromat in town, and I gave her mine, although with a nagging anxiety that I might never see them again, since she didn't seem to be sorting or labeling them very effectively. But she proved entirely trustworthy and well organized, and returned most of them that afternoon. In any case, I would have been able to do perfectly well without them, since the point of the festival turned out to be running around naked—much more so than concerts, of which all I remember are the constant warnings from the main stage admonishing the audience to use sunscreen, available at the first-aid tent, which was being overwhelmed by campers with painful nipple burns. All over the campsite, bare-assed women beat on drums or strummed guitars, while a few ran amok, with feathers in their hair and menstrual blood, or hopefully just paint, streaming down their legs. I felt lonelier than ever as I observed all this interesting and bizarre activity, wondering how someone like me would ever find her place in it, and between my work shifts in the kitchen tent scraping huge woody carrots, I made myself miserable thinking about how Cynthia and I might have amused ourselves if she had been with me. Driving home, the tollbooth attendant on the Massachusetts Turnpike who muttered, "Have a nice day," when he handed back our change was the first man any of us had spoken to in four days.

After I returned, with an all-over tan and a renewed appreciation for modern shower technology, I continued to show up dutifully at the office. But I'd reached a low point in my life. By ten o'clock my tears would be dripping onto my typewriter keys. Then I got laid off, although my boss arranged things so I could collect unemployment. I had thought the job was not important to me, just an office gig I'd taken to support my real work, *Sister Courage* and so on. But I'd been at it long enough to make a few friends, and it gave a structure to my days, and of course I needed the money. I'd arrived at the end of a certain path I'd been following: I pictured it as train tracks across a landscape. They seemed to give only the illusion of converging, but I'd reached their meeting point, possibility's end. Trapped between the rails, I had no idea what to do with myself. A friend invited to me to join her career-search support group. We sat around her kitchen table and ate cookies and complained about the hot weather and the temporary employment agencies we worked for. One member dominated several sessions telling us about her allergy to cats and the problems it had caused her. A roommate's pet had entered her room, and she'd had to throw a perfectly good futon in the trash.

Next I signed up for feminist counseling, and that's where I got some real help. The therapy group itself, which I joined because I couldn't afford individual sessions, turned out to feel too much like my huge family all over again, with the six of us kids competing for some attention from Mom. But on the bulletin board in the therapist's waiting room I saw the poster announcing the opening for a features editor at *Gay Community News*. I felt an actual shiver of destiny, like Alice Toklas, who claimed she heard the tolling of bells whenever she met a true genius, like Gertrude Stein. This according to Gertrude.

I had tacked over my desk a photograph I'd cut out from *Ms.* magazine of Gertrude and Alice, dressed for the road in coats and hats. When my sister Judith came to visit, she asked me if it was of our mother's immigrant parents—Gertrude especially, with her cropped hair and imposing nose, being a not at all implausible Ginsburg.

4

The First to Go

Gay Community News was the center of the universe. Or rather, it felt like the center of the universe. If anything, though, it was merely the center of the gay universe, a speck so obscure that it was visible from the planet of the straight people only as an occasional, annoying twinkle. Still, the *Village Voice*—an establishment paper, compared to us—once magnanimously referred to *GCN* as "the gay movement's newspaper of record," although in what context I can't imagine. I never actually saw the article but only heard it quoted by Richard at every possible opportunity, implying as it did that we were in the same category as the *New York Times*.

For example, there was the time he and I went to Provincetown for the weekend. Richard said we could crash with his aunt, who lived several towns down-Cape, and we took our bicycles on the ferry from Boston, which arrived in Provincetown at around noon. Overruling my nagging anxieties about the length of the bike ride ahead of us and the traffic on Route 6, Richard insisted on a great afternoon cruising around Commercial Street, dropping in at the Boatslip Tea Dance, and then, after I thought we'd finally gotten started, making a detour in Truro to Head of the Meadow Beach to look at the ocean. By the time we arrived at the back roads of Orleans, the sun had been down for hours, and we couldn't see each other or the road in front of us. You forget how dark it gets in the country. There were millions of stars. To help me keep track of him, Richard called back to me over and over the text of the paper's subscription form, so that like the crumbs scattered on the ground by lost children,

Members of the Fenway Gay Alliance set up this memorial on the spot where Charles Kimball was killed. Photo by John Tobin.

his words marked an ephemeral trail: "Founded in 1973 . . . lesbians and gay men . . . 52 weeks, $15 . . . no-peek envelope . . . *newspaper of record!*"

When all the illegal phone extensions in the office started ringing at once, or you glanced up and noticed the bullet holes in the front windows, you certainly felt at the center of *something.* The phone extensions were illegal because in those monopolistic days, having each one hooked up by the telephone company would have cost extra. So we paid for two phone lines, one for the advertising manager, so advertisers would never be discouraged by a busy signal, and the other for the rest of us. David Peterson, member of the original *GCN* collective, MIT graduate, and phone freak, came down to the office with a shopping bag full of handsets, adapters, and cables, and installed the extensions. David collected jars, rope, screws, beach hats, broken but possibly fixable typewriters, a majestic antique brass cash register, chairs and tables with missing legs, filing cabinets (the four-drawer in the *GCN* office labeled *homo-file* was his donation, as was the pun), mattresses, bridesmaids' dresses—and shopping bags, handsets, adapters, and cables. He owned a Victorian building of oddly laid out little apartments in Cambridge, and he later became my landlord, so I became familiar with his basement and front hallway collections. I imagined that his stuff would accumulate until it reached my apartment on the top floor, when I'd have to move out.

Each of us had two or three phones on her desk—princesses, wall units, basic black dial instruments. The phones rang constantly, and when they didn't, anyone who wanted to make me laugh could grab all of his at once, hold them to his ears and yell, "Buy! Sell!" like a Hollywood tycoon, or pick one up and bark, "City desk!" like Lou Grant on the *Mary Tyler Moore Show*. Mary was a kind of touchstone. At staff meetings, you could successfully resolve an argument by citing her: "They had a problem just like this on *Mary* once, and this is what *she* did . . ."

I worried about what would happen when a phone broke, or we decided we needed an additional legal line. David would have to dismantle the whole system before we could call in a repairman. David himself probably wouldn't have minded, since he was as interested in repairmen as all the other gay men in our office: repairmen are always humpy, they explained to me. UPS deliverymen, in their brown uniforms, even more so. They also claimed that in certain professions the practitioners were more often gay than not—they weren't talking about obvious ones like hairdresser or airline steward but about the more than statistically likely number of men they claimed to have encountered in the bushes and tearooms who were anesthesiologists, Episcopalian priests, and timpanists.

As for the bullet holes, some people, like Neil Miller, don't believe in them. He told me he never saw them, that they were another wild rumor, or at most caused by a more benign mishap—small rocks, perhaps? Of course, he hadn't been managing editor for a couple of years by the time I showed up in October 1978, so maybe the holes weren't there in his day. I remember them clearly, although, thanks to Neil, I also wonder if I made them up.

Let's say the bullet holes were real, yet symbolic. After they appeared most of the staff resignedly pushed their desks into the back of the office, except Jim Marko, the news editor, whose role as office contrarian and sex symbol somehow demanded that he rearrange his squarely in front, with his Beckett quote tacked up on the wall beside him: "I can't go on. I'll go on." Although the shooting had been perpetrated against a dark, empty space in the middle of the night—luckily no one had decided to work late or sneak back in after hours with a trick—the bullet holes reminded us every day that some people hated us. *Really* hated us.

My life hadn't prepared me for that. I was a nice girl, a good girl, a bat-mitzvah girl from the New Jersey suburbs—not the high-class suburbs, just an okay-enough place with houses and backyards and sidewalks and a miserable school system. In French class, after we finished *Le Petit Prince*, Mlle. Gradstein—my accent has never sounded like anything but New Jersey—assigned us a story about a priest or some sort of religious person who adopts a blind girl and decides, since she has no choice but to trust his account of the world around them, not to tell her about the existence of evil. She grows up, falls in love, finds out the true nature of things, and drowns herself. I wasn't about to drown myself, but in the mid-seventies, when everybody in the women's movement began talking about rape, in-cest, and battering, it all seemed so terrible and essentially *incroyable*, I knew how she felt. And then I landed at the paper, with its bullet holes, break-ins, Krazy-Glue in the door lock, bomb threats. Still, vandalism was the least of it—scary, but in the end, the office was just *stuff.*

At *GCN*, people got seriously hurt. Some died. My friends and com-rades, people I loved, or didn't, but I *knew* them, were gay-bashed, were murdered, committed suicide. Then: AIDS, AIDS, AIDS.

You can view the epidemic as discontinuous, for which nothing that came before could have prepared us—and you would not be wrong. But you can also view it as an escalation, the logical next step. Otherwise, how do you explain the fact that almost immediately we knew what to do: Yell and scream. Care for our sick. Bury our dead. No one else would do it. Across the way, in the big, straight universe, they mostly seemed unaware that anything unusual was going on, although some had seen the epidemic on TV. No one would come near us. Even the police were afraid to arrest us unless they were practically wearing hazmat suits, or at least protective gloves. We'd become hazmat, or maybe had always been.

GCN's typesetter, David Stryker, was the first to go. The first I knew.

Stryker was in his sixties? fifties? By the time I got to the paper no one knew much about who he was or where he'd come from. To me, he was a troublesome old geezer with an appalling reddish toupee, coke-bottle-thick aviator glasses, twin adolescent sons, and a nasty interest in porn and boys not much older than the twins.

Naturally, Stryker himself had a different perspective. In *GCN*'s July 1978 fifth-anniversary issue, he wrote about how proud he was of his accomplishments at the paper. For its first few issues, the collective members had typed everything onto stencils and cranked it all out on a mimeograph machine, a messy and exhausting process that took days and left them covered in ink. Then Stryker, who had worked on newspapers all his life, came around and persuaded them that it would be easier to send the paper out to be offset—although I can just hear the grumbling about how this contravened the collective principle, wherein everyone shared all tasks and no one's labor was exploited, not even that of the kids working the counter at Gnomon Copy in Harvard Square. Stryker says he went out and bought an IBM Composer—a big black contraption that looked like an oversized electric typewriter and printed the articles on roles of shiny paper, giving a somewhat sharper impression than a regular typewriter—which he set up in his living room. Ever seeking better quality, though, he immediately began lobbying for a move to a bigger press, and upgraded his own equipment from the composer to a fancy phototypesetting machine. With *GCN* as his main client he started a quixotic, doomed business—Xanadu Graphics. The day *GCN* came out printed on newsprint like a real newspaper, with justified margins and proportional spacing, was a proud one for Stryker.

He wasn't an easy man to work with. We'd hand him the week's manuscripts, and he'd hold them up an inch from his face and out to the side, squinting furiously. He had cataracts; it figures that *GCN* employed a blind typesetter. Blind and opinionated—he refused to set our copy as written. He admits in his article that one of the reasons he had wanted the paper to move beyond the "typewriter-and-mimeograph phase" was that being the typesetter would give him "full rein to fix up the spelling and grammar and syntax, because once the copy was set in type, it was difficult to make changes. Sneaky, huh?" The staff naturally saw Stryker's mangling of what he gleefully called our "deathless prose" rather differently. Some weeks we got around him by persuading one of his twins or Xanadu Graphics' ever-changing assistants to set our copy on the sly, but they began to enjoy changing it too, and like their employer started calling us on the phone to berate us about typos and ideological stupidities. On Thursday nights Stryker would show up in the middle of layout to deliver the last of the galleys and collect his check, which it eventually became my responsibility to write. He said the problem was his commitment and excessive generosity. For what we paid and the lateness of our payments, any other typesetter would refuse to work for us. But, I thought during these tirades, here he was every week, also refusing. Apart from his tirades he was man of few words and those mumbled. His mouth was peculiarly formed; like a dolphin's, it went up at the corners and made him look like he was always smiling, so I'd smile back. But he wasn't.

Eventually we decided it would be easier to typeset the paper ourselves. The father of Tom Huth, from the Thursday night layout crew, died, leaving Tom a small legacy, some of which he used to buy *GCN* a typesetting machine. So we fired Stryker, but after that, every typesetter we hired behaved exactly like him, as though he had cursed us. In fact, having the typesetters in-house was an even worse situation, because as fellow staff members they could call emergency meetings, stamp their feet, cry, and accuse the editors of undermining all that was good and beautiful and just, forever and ever.

Richard would moan, "Why can't the art department be replaced by a computer?" which actually was a pretty visionary thing to say, in the days before Quark, when we laid out the paper by hand, slicing up the long rolls of copy with exacto knives and fixing it down on the boards with sticky wax. To correct typos, our proofreading volunteer, Gordon Gottlieb—who showed up reliably every Wednesday afternoon for years, in jacket and Windsor-knotted tie, right from his office—cut out individual letters from the previous week's leftover copy, impaling the tiny *a*'s and *b*'s on the exacto knife's point and assembling them crookedly into words. Richard loved men in ties and would always greet Gordon with an enveloping hug, which Gordon tolerated. He had a neat beard and an exquisite, deadpan sense of humor. Once, watching Gordon squirm in Richard's embrace, I said, with lesbian contentiousness, "What are ties *for*, anyway? They have no purpose."

"They're because we can't wear our penises outside of our clothes," said Gordon. Much of the time, his painstaking corrections fell off the boards before they got to the printer.

By 1983, when Stryker went into the hospital, there was no one left on the staff who knew him. No one from *GCN* visited him, and his death was a rumor. It was said to have been AIDS. It was said to have been swift—as AIDS deaths were at first, beautiful gay boys shriveling up before the eyes of their baffled doctors, who in Stryker's case were deceived, perhaps, by his age into thinking his crisis was something they understood.

5

Beginnings

For a long time, I used to go to the office early.

I enjoyed the quiet of the *GCN* office in the morning, although eventually, as I began staying later and later for meetings or Thursday night layout, I began arriving later, too. Richard had an ongoing war with successive art directors about whether they were obligated to show up at all on Fridays, after supervising layout well into the early morning hours and then dropping off the paper at the printer's. He insisted that yes, they were. I thought that was unfair, and furthermore neither Richard nor anyone else was checking my work hours, but Richard said, "That's because you're here all the time, doll."

On one of those early mornings, I had hauled my bicycle up the stairs to the deserted office and was about to put it away and try to organize myself for whatever new and unfamiliar things this day would inevitably bring, when a man poked his head out from behind the *FagRag* partition. I froze. His dark hair was military-short and his face clean-shaven; he wore a light blue shirt, fat navy blue tie, pressed gray pants, spit-shined black shoes. I could think of only one thing: a policeman. In the office, poking around our stuff. And *FagRag*'s. My first ridiculous impulse was to call the cops. Then, to call Richard. Then I noticed that he didn't seem quite like a regular policeman. He seemed to know his way around.

"*Love* the hat," he said. I was still wearing my helmet. "You must be the new features dyke."

John Mitzel would come in early to do a little *FagRag* work before starting his shift as projectionist at the South Station Cinema, "Boston's

South Station and Art Cinema ads.

best all-male show"—the movies ran all day. Really he led quite a disciplined life. The cinema was one of our most faithful advertisers, and each Thursday night we pasted the week's film titles into the cinema's Gay Guy's Guide: *Size Queen* with Long Johnny Holmes, *Left Handed, Kansas City Trucking Company.* (I thought of that one during a conversation with one of our ad managers, Larry Loffredo, who after extolling his monogamous relationship had launched into a series of salacious tales about his encounters at truckstops in the Midwest. "But Larry, I thought you said you were monogamous," I interrupted. He looked at me with surprise. "Not outside Route 128, hon.") The titles changed regularly, although I began to wonder whether the films did. Watching the movie, I learned, wasn't exactly the point of the South Station Cinema.

Although before coming to the paper I had been vaguely aware that some gay men groped each other in public bathrooms, my image of the kinds of people who would engage in such activities had come mostly from watching *The Boys in the Band*—pathetic closet cases living self-destructive, distorted lives. The movie had made me feel like a voyeur, and even though I was watching it alone, on late-night TV, I kept pretending to myself that I was about to turn it off—actually I was fascinated and watched it right through to poor Harold's suicide and the credits. Around the same time I read a memoir by a gay activist in which he recounted having a lot of sex in the New York Port Authority bus terminal, but all that changed once he came out and discovered he could instead have mature loving relationships with men he met at Gay Activists Alliance dances.

So although I tried to be cool and never once blurted, "You *what?*" I was often shocked at the morning chat of the men with whom I was working about what they had done the evening before at the cinema, in the Fenway Victory Gardens, in the Harvard Science Center bathrooms, in the back room at Herbie's Ramrod bar. Sometimes, telling these stories, they used female pronouns and called each other Mary. It all seemed much more retrograde than the image I'd formed of gay liberation from my reading and my observation of the men's collective that did volunteer child care at women's music concerts, the gentle-looking, long-haired couples holding hands at the gay pride march, the *GCN* classified ad calling together a gay men's discussion group on class, contact Clover or Cha-Cha. I'd gotten the idea that Stonewall had done away with anonymous sex—although the notion that rioting bar patrons would have had that as their goal shows my lack of insight.

The cover story of the first issue of *GCN* that I worked on was one of the rare triumphant ones—the defeat of California's Briggs Initiative, Proposition 6. If the initiative, propagated by state senator John Briggs, had passed, it would have required firing any teacher, administrator, or worker, right down to the janitor, in a public school who was suspected of being lesbian or gay—or even of mentioning the words. The tactic that defeated this idiotic proposal—but didn't prevent similar ones from being repeatedly introduced in other states to this very day—was coming out. Gay Californians had simply introduced themselves to their neighbors. They'd handed out flyers in shopping malls and laudromats—"I am GAY"—which was incredibly courageous of them; I'd hesitate to do it even now. Then there was Mitzel's perspective, which he presented in a long tirade in *GCN*'s op-ed column, Speaking Out: "I regard myself as a victim of the Amerikan public education system," he wrote.

Just to argue the point, it would be *more* radical (and considerably more pro-student—and who has thought about *them* in this fray?) for the Left to advocate *passing* Prop. 6, then organizing the students to report every teacher and administrator. . . . It would not only *close down the schools* during the investigations of the accused (letting the kids surf and do dope), but at an estimated $40,000 to investigate each and every complaint, it would *bankrupt the state of California!*

Although I felt Mitzel's logic was somehow faulty, I couldn't quite come up with a counterargument. Mitzel occasionally wrote letters to *GCN*, which were signed by his alter ego, Bunny LaRue, but this column was bylined "Mitzel," like his news stories, which I interpret to mean that he was, although perhaps only on a deep and inaccessible level, serious about his utopia of a withered-away state populated by stoned surfer boys. Or rather, like Mitzel's clothing style, the article was both serious and an enraged joke. Although the effect of his attire was that of a uniform, the service represented by Mitzel would have been hard to define.

His uniform was really the opposite of a uniform, since he was the only person who wore it, in contrast to the Castro Street Clone look that had begun to appear everywhere, although not so much in the *GCN* office. The clones wore flannel shirts—fitted and carefully pressed, nothing like baggy Goodwill lesbian ones—button-fly, Levi's 501 shrink-to-fit jeans, and heavy orange work boots, annoying everyone with their plaid conformity. Was this what gay liberation had come to? we slovenly dressers asked, already nostalgic for a lost golden age. A gym membership, a mustache, and an account with L.L. Bean, that old fascist? We couldn't decide whether the clones were obnoxiously masculine, with their muscles and facial hair, or fey, in their strict observance of fashion guidelines. The questions raised by the new style were similar to those raised by the leather fetishists, with their glowering looks and fearsome studded gear, who were also accused of trying to look like straight men, although for me this line of thinking was forever shattered by Charley Shively's observation, "What straight man would wear a hat like that?"—black leather with a little peak and an ornamental chain across the bill. At one point I got into trouble (self-hating! homophobic!) for running an article on the whole clone/leather phenomenon that the author had titled "He Looks Like Tarzan but He Talks Like Jane," in which he complained that even the most leathery of tops at the bar just wanted to exchange cake recipes.

BIPAD: 65498

ISSN: 0147-0728

gay community news

VOL. 6, NO. 15   NOVEMBER 4, 1978   THE GAY WEEKLY 50¢

GAY RIGHTS

REGISTER & VOTE

FOR RENT 759-3175

VILLAGE CARS

RICO

Hatch
vs
King
in Mass.
Election

Larry
Berner:
Teacher
Fights Back

S.F.
Bath Fire
Kills One

SPECIAL ISSUE ON BRIGGS INITIATIVE

Although Mitzel fascinated me, with his outrageous opinions and wit and unusual habits, I never really got to know him. I don't think anyone did, with the possible exception of Michael Bronski, who used to visit with him regularly most Fridays and still does, first at the cinema, and then, when that closed, at the Glad Day gay bookstore that opened across the hall from *GCN*, and finally at Mitzel's own business venture, Calamus Books, named for the Walt Whitman poem cycle and specializing in pornographic videotapes.

Bronski himself wrote prolifically, even obsessively, for *GCN*, churning out incredibly smart, misspelled articles, interviews, entire series, and book, film, and theater reviews—which I greatly appreciated, since it was never easy to find writers for a publication that imposed weekly deadlines yet paid absolutely nothing. Although some *GCN* writers managed to fit in their assignments during weekends, evenings, and vacations, most were un- or underemployed, temporarily or chronically. My first encounter with Bronski was not promising. Eric had left me a card file of writers, through which I was working my way, and when I called Bronski to introduce myself, he had answered the phone warily.

"Can I speak to Michael Bronski?"

"Michael? Who? Bronski?" Michael said. "He's—I—he's indisposed."

I knew this was fishy, even though I'd never spoken to him before. "Ask him to call me at *GCN*."

"Oh thank god," said Michael, dropping the facade. "I thought you were a caseworker." The reason he had so much time to write for *GCN* was that he had convinced the Social Security and food stamp bureaucrats that he was too mentally ill to work, simply by confirming their assumptions about crazy faggots. Among other problems, he claimed he couldn't leave his apartment, because he was afraid he'd be beaten by queer bashers. And in fact, except to drop off articles at the *GCN* office or pick up men at the Ramrod, he preferred not to venture far from Cambridge, where he lived with Walta Borawski, his lover.

They invited me to countless dinners at their apartment, where bookshelves lined the walls not only in every room but also in the front hall, with books and record albums arranged at least two layers deep. Music was always playing—Nina Simone and Billie Holiday and Maria Callas, of course, but also more obscure singers, whom Michael and Walta were forever discovering and loving—and all evening, to illustrate various conversational points, they would pull down books from the shelves. Michael read everything and probably has a more sophisticated understanding of feminism than I can ever aspire to, so he was I think genuinely hurt when *GCN* received angry letters from both Adrienne Rich and Audre Lorde objecting to his use of a quote from Audre in an article about S&M— although both he and I were also totally thrilled to discover they read the paper. Rich said the quote was "a wrenching out of context which feels to me like rape." Walta, in his letter leaping to the defense of Michael's (and presumably their mutual) sexual practices, said this extreme characterization emptied the word "rape" of almost all meaning—a rhetorical maneuver that was downright "*manly*" of Rich, he concluded.

Mitzel, too, wrote book reviews and other features for *GCN*, so I would occasionally have to call him to negotiate the edits, which he usually refused to take. Each time, I felt supremely uncomfortable, a female voice intruding into his home. Mitzel himself never answered but had to be called to the phone, and I found it difficult to imagine someone so completely sui generis living with a roommate from the want ads or a lover or a gay collective, like the rest of us.

Several years after I left the paper, I heard that Mitzel's landlord had sold the building he lived in, and that he had moved in with Robert Etherington—or Etheringperson, as Gregg and Harry Seng dubbed him—a sometime *GCN* writer and proofreader. Robert was a dedicated opera aficionado who wore a cloak for his forays into the office and had worked forever in the Harvard Coop record department, where I now suspect he acted as an accessory to Bronski's shoplifting missions. Bronski never acknowledged Robert as an accomplice, preferring you to think he had gotten away with the albums through sheer talent and daring, and maybe he had. They were always presents for Walta, more of an opera queen than anyone, as well as a lover of Barbra Streisand, despite the reluctantly negative review he had written of one of her albums, which had provoked a letter to the editor that said, essentially, "Who are *you*, Worm, to criticize *Barbra?*" Bronski would admit only to having run into Robert and been provoked by him into a long, pointless disagreement about the merits of various sopranos. Robert was said to be a Republican, or as much of one as a *GCN* writer could aspire to be, and Mitzel was a total anarchist, so I assume the Mitzel–Etheringperson arrangement was one of convenience, and that the two of them had little interaction—but for me it detracts a little from the mystique of each to have to imagine him in his room, and the labels on the milk cartons in the refrigerator.

During my first few months of coming in early to *GCN*, Richard would arrive at the office not long after I did—it would still be another hour or so before the place got really crowded—carrying a dripping paper cup of coffee and a *Times*, his hair slicked back from the shower. Mitzel, still scuttling around in the *FagRag* area, would poke his head out, look Richard over, and say, "What did you do, swim here, girlfriend?" His *FagRag* work apparently finished, he would grab a small duffle bag and take his leave: "Ta-ta kids, got to get to the gym before the drugs wear off."

6

The Saints and Somewhere

The dispute was over a news article. But I had nothing to do with news articles, although trying to explain this to anyone outside of the paper would have been disloyal, I felt, not to mention fruitless. I was the features editor, which meant that all I knew in advance about the news were the week's headlines, gleaned from the news editor's report at the Tuesday morning staff meeting. And a lot of that was wishful thinking, if not deliberate obfuscation, since *GCN* news editors generally resented going to the staff meeting, which they viewed as wasted time. As far as they were concerned, the news was the news, and discussion of it simply a refusal to accept reality. So I didn't see the news articles until they came out in the paper, just like anyone else. And sometimes while I was reading them, sitting at my desk on a quiet Friday afternoon, after the printer's van had delivered the papers, and I had helped to carry the bundles up the stairs, and the early-bird Folders had begun to trickle in to sort address lists and organize envelopes, I would get a terrible feeling in the pit of my stomach.

The biggest problem with the article should not have been that it mentioned The Saints bar. The Saints was not merely peripheral to the story, it was totally irrelevant. The brawl happened outside of the *other* lesbian bar, Somewhere, which was around the corner from The Saints and a different scene altogether, even though just about everyone who went to The Saints also patronized Somewhere. If you were deliberately planning to end up at Somewhere—as opposed to just poking your head in the door before closing to make sure you hadn't missed anything after an evening at The Saints—you dressed differently. Hipper, sexier. My Somewhere

The Saints Collective. From left: *Donna Boucher, Donna Senay, Merry Moscato, Sandra Monroe, and Sandra Goings.*

jeans were a pair my younger sister had been about to throw out, which were impractical for daily wear. I didn't quite have to lie down to zip them, but almost. Somewhere was a lesbian pleasure palace, with three floors and separate areas for dancing, for playing pool, for intimate conversation, and for listening to live music—the story is that Tracy Chapman auditioned, but after hearing her routine one of the bartenders, in an episode of spectacularly bad judgment, told her to forget about a musical career. Or, alternatively, that one of Tracy's first professional gigs was at Somewhere, and she wowed the audience, who immediately sensed that she would go on to bigger things. Each of the three floors had its own bar, where, if you were like me, you could sit and watch all the women dancing, playing pool, listening to music, and coming together and apart all evening in different configurations.

But Somewhere was a later development in the Boston lesbian scene. In the beginning was The Saints. That is, unless you count Jacques, a drag bar with a scary reputation that admitted lesbians during the inchoate pre-Saints era, I guess on the theory that everyone there would have a common interest in presenting herself as a woman one way or another— although, proving Simone DeBeauvoir's adage that a woman is made and not born, the drag queens were generally more successful than the lesbians.

I never went to Jacques. I belong to the proud generation that came out in The Saints, which some people will tell you was the best lesbian bar anywhere, ever. The Saints was managed by The Saints collective: Donna (pronounced by Bostonians *Dawn-uh*), Merry, Sandy, and Sandra. A lot of groups called themselves collectives in those days, including us at *GCN*, but The Saints collective was like the Beatles in *A Hard Day's Night*, in the scene where each Beatle goes into a separate doorway, and then in the next shot you see that they all end up together in the same living room. The Saints shared an apartment and ran the bar together, and some of them were lovers, too, although I didn't know them well enough to be sure of who matched up with whom. I was a thoroughly anonymous patron of the bar, until I started working for *GCN* and the news article came out, and I became notorious.

The bar was inconveniently located on a side street in the dark, confusing Financial District. At first I got rides with friends, then I figured out how to walk there from the subway station; but I never lost the feeling that I'd found the place by lucky accident, as though it were a kind of Brigadoon. The story went that Sandy, who had been a daytime waitress there, convinced the owner that he'd make a lot more money if, instead of closing up when his banker clientele went home, he let her open the place at night for her lesbian friends. Every once in a while a lesbian unaware of this arrangement would decide to check out her favorite bar for lunch, only to find herself surrounded by a crowd of guys in suits; and similarly from time to time a guy in a suit, who had perhaps been intrigued by the graffiti in the bathroom, would turn up of an evening. He was never refused service and usually left without finishing his beer.

Cops, too, showed up occasionally, in uniform or out, claiming they were required to enforce certain laws for our own protection, such as the venerable one that forbade dancing without a permit. Now, many of us at The Saints were clumsy though enthusiastic dancers, and it may be that we got worse as the night wore on, but it's not like we were truly dangerous. The cops would unplug the jukebox, and everyone would crowd into the front room around the bar, waiting to see if the place was finally going to be raided or shut down—and I worried that we would have to riot, like at Stonewall. Being physically timid, I didn't look forward to throwing chairs and being arrested. These visitations to The Saints always ended peacefully, though, with whispered negotiations between the cops and the collective, after which the cops would get a free drink and whatever other gratuity they required.

The Saints took its name from a stained-glass artwork behind the bar, which was usually tended by Merry and Donna, while Sandy and Sandra worked the door. Merry had the convivial personality you'd expect in a bartender, but Donna was utterly taciturn. One Halloween she dressed as a fairy princess, with a tutu and a pair of gauzy wings. The straps of her yellow leotard slipped off her thin shoulders as she reached across the bar to hand you your drink, and her face below her sparkly tiara was as solemn as Grant Wood's farmer's.

The Saints consisted of three wood-paneled rooms: the front room, with the bar to the right, an island in the center, and several pinball machines to the left of the door; a side room with booths and a pool table; and in the very back, the dance floor. The place had a sort of emotional geography, each room with its particular terrain crowded with women familiar and unfamiliar, offering different possibilities every few feet. The night to go to The Saints was Wednesday, even though of course most people had to work the next day. I thought of it as yet another challenge of living as a lesbian in a hostile world. On some Wednesdays I never advanced past the front room, it was so crowded with people I knew, or wanted to know, and there was so much to say to all of them, even for a generally tongue-tied person like me. That was the magic of it. At The Saints we were all intriguing, we were all desirable, we were all stars, even though in the rest of the world we were dorks and loners—queers, in fact. Late in the even-ing, when I had been dancing for hours, hugging briefly one woman then another, jumping up and down, music blasting— Patti LaBelle, *"Voulez-vous couchez avec moi / ce soir"*—a moment would come when I would feel ecstatic with love for everyone, *every single one of us,* all of us lesbians together, even if I didn't have anyone to go home with.

The Saints collective were zealously if not insanely protective of their creation. They allowed *GCN* to list The Saints in the paper's bar guide, on the condition that we print no information except its name and a phone number which, with an appealing circularity, was the number of the *GCN* office. Women callers were to be given the address, directions, and hours; men were to be told we had no idea what they were talking about. The secrecy gave The Saints an exclusive aura that was a sort of cross between speakeasy and Boston Brahmin heiress, whose name, it was said, should appear in the newspaper only on the occasions of her birth, marriage, and death.

And certainly not in connection with a brawl, even when the only person who ended up in the hospital was the guy who started it, outside of Somewhere—*not* The Saints —by trying to push over some motorcycles parked outside. The bouncer told him to quit it, and his attitude was "yeah, make me," and suddenly there were a million lesbians pouring out of the bar, and he and his buddies and their dates and the lesbians were all punching and kicking one another and throwing bottles and stuff. Some people said the bar manager ordered the doors locked to keep the aggressors outside, thus leaving the lesbians no escape route; but others said no way, the lesbians retreated into the bar to safety. The cops didn't show up until the whole thing was over, and there was nothing much left to do but transport the injured to the emergency room—even though, according to the *GCN* article about the incident, the police had been summoned throughout the fight, three times from Somewhere and once from The Saints.

That's what started the controversy—which was not, as you might think, about the indifference of the police. It was about the fact that *GCN* printed the name of The Saints, in a context that might enable an attentive reader to deduce the bar's location. My personal opinion has always been that it wasn't The Saints collective but Ann Maguire, the manager of Somewhere, who was most justified in being incredibly pissed off, since the article had been illustrated, in the desperation of Thursday night layout, with an unfortunate file photo of her frowning fiercely over the headline, "Women Beaten at Somewhere." Actually, the photo was a blow-up of a detail from a group shot, and you know how there's always at least one person making a funny face when the shutter clicks? Readers glancing at the front page might easily have concluded that Ann, who appeared to be a maniac, had done the beating. The article did little to dispel the confusion, consisting as it did of a string of quotes from the participants and the police, with no apparent effort made to create a chronology, reconcile contradictions, or assess the reliability of the various accounts. Despite our best efforts, these kinds of problems were typical of *GCN* news stories, which were written by inexperienced volunteers on tight deadlines. Usually, annoyed readers wrote in with corrections, follow-up coverage was provided, and eventually either some kind of truth emerged, or something else happened that grabbed everyone's attention.

But The Saints controversy was of another order. On the Tuesday night after the article appeared, the collective held a big, rowdy emergency meeting, which drew about two hundred regulars and friends. I wasn't invited. The next night, Wednesday, only vaguely aware that something was up, I went to the bar as usual. I didn't want my absence to give the impression that *GCN* had something to hide. Since I'd begun working at the paper, I had more than once been handed messages for other staffers or had checks for classified ads stuffed into my pocket during an evening out. I'd become completely identified in people's minds with *Gay Community News*, no matter what I said or did. Anyway, on a personal level, I knew that staying home would be the start of a slide down a slippery slope, which would end with my abandoning any remaining pretense to a social life. Not going to The Saints would eventually mean not going anywhere at all. And if you missed even a few weeks at the bars, you felt exiled—like Marcia Womongold, a local antipornography crusader notorious for having shot up the window display in the Reading International bookstore in Harvard Square because they carried magazines like *Playboy*. She wrote to *GCN* about being kicked out of *Somewhere*—unjustly, she said:

Dears,

I would like the community to judge my situation with regard to the bar, Somewhere, purportedly a "women's" bar.

Last July 4, I unfortunately fired off teargas in the men's room at Somewhere. I had been celebrating by firing off blanks, and had reloaded my starter pistol for the walk home. After a few drinks, I forgot the gun was loaded with teargas and fired it off in a moment of jovial stupidity as I was relaxing in the men's room. No one else was in the room at the time, but imagine my chagrin when a cloud of teargas drifted around me and I realized my error.

When the noxious odor was detected by the staff, I apologized. Ann Maguire, the manager, very understandably banned me from the bar for six months. But after waiting out the six month exile, I returned to Somewhere on Jan. 4, only to be insulted, bullied, and told I could consider myself banned for five years, in other words, forever.

As a gay woman, this leaves me very little leeway in my social activities, since our options are few to begin with. I resent Maguire's reneging on our original agreement without explanation. I was insulted and my actions were called "inhuman." In other words, an armed woman is less than human (having rejected the role of passive victim). On the very night of my confrontation with Maguire, I was followed from Washington Station all the way to Somewhere by five drunken men howling for "cunt." Women have been raped and beaten in the area, and arming ourselves is a proof of our self-love and our readiness to defend our sisters. It's time we lesbians stop oppressing each other.

Fondly,
Marcia Womongold

(Bunny LaRue wrote in the following week to suggest that the issue could be resolved amicably if lesbians would simply agree, as in the Wild West, to check weapons at the door.)

When I arrived at The Saints, Sandra greeted me by name at the door, which I found quite flattering, since I hadn't realized she knew who I was. Telling Sandy she'd be back shortly, she stood up and walked me inside. I'd never before realized how tall she was. She handed me a letter. It had been passed around at the community meeting and personally endorsed by everyone there.

"This goes in the next issue," she said, towering above me in a corner next to a bleeping pinball machine. "With every single signature."

"I don't see how we can make space for all this," I squeaked, flipping through the pages. The paper was crumpled, and some of the names were totally illegible; it was a letter written in a bar, after all. "Can't we just print some—"

"You have just received a non-negotiable demand, baby. We've got nothing to talk about." Sandra dismissed me and went back to her post.

After that it was hard to work up to my usual bar-night ecstasy. The women surrounding me, whom I'd loved so much, had signed the letter. I'd become the enemy, apparently even more than the motorcycle-pushing, bottle-throwing, lesbian-punching thugs who'd started the fight. Standing alone at the island in the front room with a beer, trying to figure out what to do with myself, I noticed the throng at the door parting to let someone through: Ann Maguire. It was incongruous to see her outside of

Ann Maguire.
Photo by Susan Fleischmann.

Vol. 7, No. 47 (617) 426-44

Ann Maguire
Susan Fleischmann

Women Beaten At Somewhere

By Marie Cartier

BOSTON—"Someone knocked me over, and then a foot at the velocity of the speed of light came at me when I tried to get up," said Aileen O'Neill, one of approximately two dozen women who were assaulted in front of the Boston women's bar, Somewhere, Friday night, June 6. "All I could see was this white sneaker, then I saw stars."

Another man, identified by police as Marc Kelley, 18, also of Dorchester, was at this time "getting particularly antsy with my bike," said the Somewhere staffer. "I told him to keep off the bike, and he said 'You gonna make me?' By this time there was another woman outside with me. She told Kelley to leave the bike alone. Deano walked over to her. We thought he was going to say

Somewhere, especially in The Saints. As she made her way across the room, I wondered what she was doing there. Then she stopped right in front of me. She looked almost as terrifying as she had in her photograph.

"Someone told me I could find you here," she said. She had a copy of the paper. "This so-called news article—"

"Oh," I said. "Ann. I—"

Despite the article's terrible and probably completely unjustified account of Ann, I felt that loyalty to the paper and to the staff required that I not repudiate or even criticize the piece. And I couldn't apologize—it wasn't mine to apologize for. Nor could I commit to doing anything to make up for it. I couldn't think of a thing to say. It wouldn't surprise me to discover that I fainted dead away at that point or, like the Cowardly Lion confronted by Oz, fled the building, barking and waving my arms.

Ann has long since moved on from managing a bar. She became a political leader in Boston, the official city liaison to the gay and lesbian community and later the deputy mayor. Whenever she sees me she greets me with a kiss and a hearty handshake. Her girlfriend once recommended me for a job. I've gone to parties at their house. But it was years before I could meet her eyes, and even now I hope she doesn't read this and decide to come looking for me again.

This is the letter Sandra handed me, which Ann had endorsed as well:

We would like to object to the article in GCN *headlined "Women Beaten at Somewhere." The sensationalistic tone of this article did not show any respect for victims of the violent attack or the process that followed the attack. Writers for* GCN *were asked by staff members of The Saints and Somewhere and other women at the Saturday morning courthouse hearing to wait to print the information concerning the June 6th attack in order for the article to accurately and respectfully portray the actual events of this incident.*

Following the attack a community meeting was held and no reporters from GCN *identified themselves at that meeting. Without accurate information as to the subsequent developments generated by the community meeting at which there were over 200 concerned women present,* GCN *could not possibly have printed any story that reflected the truth of this situation. There were many factual errors throughout the article. Therefore the undersigned are demanding a retraction and follow up coverage concerning the events of June 6th and the response from the community concerning ways in which to proceed from here.*

We would like to make it clear to our sisters in Boston and across the country that we are dealing in a strong and effective way with the safety of women in our community.

It's true that one reason we loved *The Saints* was that it was safe. The two Sandras did their best to keep the police and the owner and other creeps away from us, and inside the bar they stopped most fights before they started. If a woman was drunk or high, or simply heedless or depressed, *The Saints* women made sure she had a ride home or someone to walk her to the train. Donna and Merry were just as happy to sell you a soda as a beer, which cost fifty cents. You didn't have to declare yourself a butch or a femme or anything in particular, although you could if you wanted to. You didn't have to dress up, but a suit and tie would not get you thrown out on the street. (Through the seventies and probably in some desolate places even now, gay bars, with the backing of police, enforced an anti-drag rule that patrons had to be wearing at least three items of gender-appropriate clothing—and the police weren't shy about scrutinizing any garments, undergarments, or accessories they deemed ambiguous.)

But there's something else, although I hesitate to bring it up: Although the letter expressed a lot of righteous indignation about inaccuracies and omissions in the article, it didn't explain exactly what they were. Maybe the problem was that the event was confusing, the article even more so, and the more time passed, the less anyone was going to be able to untangle it all. But it's hard to banish entirely the suspicion that what prompted the bars to call the meeting was not only safety but profitability, and that one purpose of the meeting had been to preemptively distract people with *GCN*'s faults, heading off anyone who might note the bars' interest in suppressing information about the fight, with its potential to frighten away customers.

Richard ran the letter over the names of Ann and The Saints collective, with an editor's note acknowledging that 121 additional people had also signed it. The note also explained that the *GCN* staff had felt it important to publish a timely article in order to dispel rumors and calm fears, and that we welcomed additional corrections and information. Strangely, this seems to have satisfied everyone, because we never heard another thing about it.

When I ventured back to The Saints, after a month or so, everyone in the collective welcomed me and from then on were unfailingly friendly. We had weathered a crisis together, but they apparently or maybe generously forgot exactly what our respective roles in it had been, sort of like what happens when you run into the woman your girlfriend had an affair with years before. The girlfriend is long gone, and the affair too is in the distant past, and you can't quite remember how you know this person except for a sense that the two of you once shared an interest. So you feel a kinship, a warmth. Only later do you recall the particular interest you shared, and that she was ruining your life.

Some say that the lesbian community is a romantic myth. But during the seventies and eighties, Boston had, in addition to the bars, the Women's Center, two successive women's restaurants (Bread and Roses, which then became Amaranth), women's folk music concerts, women's theater festivals, a women's softball league, women's art shows, a women's symphony orchestra that performed works by women (I briefly played second violin), International Women's Day celebrations, New Words (the best women's bookstore in the country), three women's newspapers, a women's adult education school—it was all called "women's," but everybody knew that meant "lesbian"—and the late great women's nude swim at the Cambridge YWCA. You were required to wear a bathing cap, but anything else was optional, causing a moment of panic when you stepped over the threshold between locker room and pool, squinting around myopically, unable to discern whether the other swimmers indeed had no suits on—was that a blur of red pubic hair or a tiny bright bikini? You were living out the classic nightmare of being unclothed in public, until you dove into the cool, cloudy water, which caressed you *all over.* The pool at the Y is closed now, like everything else, except the women's center and the softball teams.

Many of us—or at least I—believed that our institutions were not so much "alternative" or "underground" as harbingers of a great cultural shift, and would eventually replace the old, outmoded symphonies, bookstores, newspapers, and so forth. But even in their heyday, they never had enough money or volunteers, and there were constant internal squabbles, and then some new lesbians coming up muttered that women's folk music was boring, and they didn't see the point of a women's restaurant especially if the food wasn't all that great. I admit that one night my dinner companion complained that her dessert was burnt, and the waitresses and cooks gathered around our table and passed it around—"Doesn't taste burnt to me"; "Nope, me neither"—and refused to take it off the bill.

Our community institutions contained the seeds of their own destruction even as they blossomed. I can get nostalgic and regretful, but in some ways, they were not that different from the ones they were supposed to replace. The people they served best were exactly those like me: white, educated, young, childless, able-bodied, politically aware and engaged. Middle class. Blithely privileged. Able to pass, if it came down to that, unless we were doing something like actively making out on the subway—as Urvashi liked to do, and then if a guy tried to start anything, she would retort, "Suck my cock!" which generally stopped the taunter cold, giving us time to leap out of the car at the next stop. But what about lesbians who were poor, who were black or Asian or Latina, who were bringing up kids—what about their needs for friendship and affirmation and art and political engagement? The community I was so proud of attracted few such women, although women of color were more visible in projects like homeless shelters and battered women's shelters and women's health clinics and rape crisis centers and prisoner support groups. Interestingly, many of these service groups are still around, even as the lesbian cultural community has faded away. Of course, after twenty or thirty years, there have been changes—the clinics are affiliated with hospitals, the collectives have been replaced by executive directors and boards, the volunteers have gone to school and become social workers. Cities and states and even the federal government provide funding. The grassroots movement became a profession; you could get a PhD in it. But social service organizations are not the same as community and culture.

Still, we were not *only* white, *only* young, etc. Am I guilty here of once again blotting out the contributions of women of color—as people like me have done so many times before? Even among the women's music concerts, for example, were events like the Varied Voices of Black Women, a national tour of poets and musicians. It was a great celebration, and we lesbians were proud to have brought the tour to Boston, despite the city's terrible reputation after the busing crisis of the 1970s, sparked when the courts required the city to desegregate its schools, and the stonings, riots, beatings, and hateful white faces spewing invective every night on the national news. That concert was standing room only, but I had managed to get tickets for myself and my sister Rebecca, who had come for a visit that weekend. She was sixteen, and every time I glanced at her sitting beside me she was stony-faced, even through all the cheering and the ovations. But she's not someone who reveals her emotions easily, or at all, so maybe she was not as uncomfortable as she looked. Maybe she was actually enjoying herself. Maybe when she came out as a lesbian many years later she remembered that evening and thanked me, mentally, for taking her with me. I like to think it's a possibility.

Varied Voices later generated a small controversy when it turned out that one of the musicians had a man playing in her backup band. Some fans said that simply by definition it could not be women's music with a man on bass. Others countered that the expectation that women's music be performed exclusively by women was racist, in that it reduced black women musicians to only one dimension of identity, when in fact they had perfectly good reason to wish to develop their art with other black people as well as with other women. Or with anyone at all who had the chops.

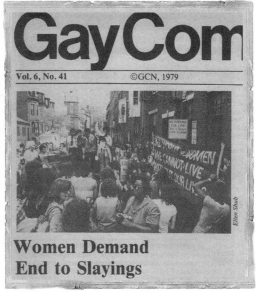

Women Demand
End to Slayings

Well, if lesbians didn't analyze these sorts of things, who would? Politically, everyone knew we could be counted on. In Boston we marched for the integration of the schools and to protect the black families and students. We were antinuke, antiwar, pro–reproductive rights. We swelled the picket lines any time there was a strike. In 1979, the Combahee River Collective, a group of black lesbians, called upon everyone in the city to mobilize around a series of murders of black women—but initially it was mostly lesbians who actually showed up. When the protests started, four women had been killed; in the end, a year later, there were thirteen murders, most never solved. The police insisted for many months that there was no connection among the deaths, and when the story of yet another attack appeared in the newspaper, it was nothing but little squib on an inside page, as though it had barely happened, as though the woman had never quite existed in the first place. Combahee led marches to the murdered women's homes and places of work and to the neighborhoods where they had been killed—parts of the city I had never ventured into before.

The violence and official indifference were terrifying and depressing, but the passion of the demonstrations was uplifting. We marched behind the Combahee banner, "We Cannot Live Without Our Lives," a line from a poem by Barbara Deming, who was white, which I took to mean that other white people, even I, might have something to contribute to the struggle. Antiracism workshops became all the rage in the lesbian community. I went to one at the Harriet Tubman House, a community center in the multiracial South End, to which I needed bus directions—the organizers having realized that the first thing to do was to move us out of our familiar, comfy spaces like the Women's Center. The workshop was nothing like the ones I was required to attend later, in connection with various jobs, which were facilitated by well-paid professionals who drew diagrams with colored markers on big sheets of newsprint, and which usually culminated in paroxysms of guilt and self-righteousness. This one and the others that followed were free-form; you never knew what you'd come up with. At the Tubman House, we decided to temporarily break into small affinity groups, and not knowing quite where I fit in—I wasn't working class or a single parent or black—I went to the Jewish women's circle. The Jewish women took turns introducing themselves, and after the last of the Shumkins and Cohens and Mermelsteins, there was a confused pause. One Jewish name after another—counting the occasional Goldman transmogrified to Womongold (why was it so often the Jewish women who cast off their patriarchal surnames?)—it was unexpectedly moving. We carried all the old, Lower East Side names, but we were the next generation, and this led into a discussion about anti-Semitism, and growing up in the fifties with the Holocaust barely in the past, and the persistence of prejudice of all kinds. (Names like ours were not heard every day in Yankee New England, and a friend of mine who grew up in Dorchester once told me, "For us, Israel wasn't the Promised Land. New York was.") Meanwhile, the black women met in one big group, separately from the white women, although afterward, when we came back together to discuss our experiences, one said the format had made her nervous: "When I saw all you white people whispering together, all I could think was, 'What are they getting up to *now*?'"

Separation. Integration. Neither seemed to solve anything. One of the underlying assumptions of the workshop had been that black identity trumped any other, and that while the whites might be sorted and re-sorted on the basis of various parameters, the black women all belonged together. But as with the musicians, this caused immediate problems, since of course no one is just one thing, so for example if you were a black, lesbian, lower middle class, college-educated, West Coast jazz pianist, where exactly would that put you? My niece recently showed me the toolbar on her computer screen, with its array of tiny icons. As you move the cursor across them, each icon in turn inflates and zooms out at you. This hallucinatory effect is perhaps not a bad metaphor for identity, with its elements and functions constantly emerging from and retreating into the background, except with identity it's not in any kind of order but somehow all at once.

Eventually, because of the demonstrations and the workshops and even the Varied Voices, I began to feel less utopian about the lesbian community. Away with separatism, I decided, of all kinds! It always seemed to come down to high-schoolish hairsplitting: who was in and who out, who up and who down, and whether transsexuals were allowed in the Women's Center, and if not would you have to do random panty-checks? The lesbian community, of all communities, could surely go beyond that, growing broader and more complicated and more contradictory and more weird and admitting that it sometimes burned the dessert—but wait a minute, then would *lesbian* mean anything at all? Maybe not, but the community would be so big and beautiful it wouldn't matter. *Everybody* would be a lesbian, as we had sung along with Lavender Jane, although I suppose that wasn't quite what they had meant.

I wangled a meeting with one of the Combahee members, Lorraine Bethel, to see if she'd do some writing for *GCN* and encourage her friends to do the same. She seemed friendly and interested, but after that, whenever I called her she never had the time. Later, she published a poem called "What Chou Mean *We*, White Girl?"—one of the points of which she had tried to explain more mildly to me during our conversation: that increasing diversity at *GCN*, and in the whole lesbian community, was my white girl's mission, not hers, she had her own problems. Of course, if all black lesbians felt that way, then *GCN* and our community would never change; but maybe that was her point too. It was the nature of the enterprise from the very beginning; it didn't touch her.

Somehow, out of all this, I developed an odd belief in a kind of mirror-community of bars, concerts, theater companies, and the like among black lesbians (as if the community I had enjoyed were the only kind possible) and began to insist that *GCN*, myself included, was not doing enough to "find" these third-world institutions. Wishfully, I imagined that if only I were invited to the right neighborhood, to the right party, with the right people—like Lorraine—I'd discover them. ("Discover" as in Columbus,

I suppose, although I surely didn't think of it that way then.) It would be so cool. I would be so warmly welcomed, an antiracist pioneer. There were always black writers and volunteers at *GCN*, but I began to wonder if they were the *right* black people, because they seemed to know nothing about the "black gay community" of my political fantasies, which of course remained elusive.

Gay bars, like all our other institutions, came and went. The Saints could not last forever. In 1981, its owner decided that if a bunch of dykes could make money running his bar at night, surely he could do even better with a heterosexual country-western theme. It never really caught on, though. Meanwhile the collective spent several years wandering in the wilderness, throwing rent parties to raise the money to reopen in a space of their own. They finally gave up when a new generation arose that knew nothing of The Saints and in any case didn't get bent out of shape if a guy appeared in their favorite club. They didn't refer to him as *a prick*, as in, "A prick just walked in the door."

Lightning just doesn't strike twice, although Merry is running a pleasant little café, everybody welcome, down the street from where the women's bookstore used to be. The food's pretty good.

7

Over the Rainbow

When all of us from *GCN* decided to travel to Washington, D.C., in October 1979 for the first ever lesbian and gay march on the capital, all I could think about was my politico-moral dilemma about where to stay. Richard's college roommate, who lived in Washington, had invited Richard to stay at his house, and Richard said I should come too, we'd have a blast. He was probably right, but during this important national milestone, I felt my rightful place to be not with him but with lesbians. A few weeks before the march, in The Saints, *GCN*'s local reporter/circulation manager, Jil Clark, had struck up a conversation with a woman who had turned out to be an Irish diplomat stationed in Washington. The diplomat had said that although she couldn't march for fear of losing her job, and in fact had arranged to be as far from Washington as possible that weekend, she wanted to support her sisters by inviting Jil to crash in her apartment while she was gone. So Jil was going around asking every lesbian she could find to stay there with her. She urged me to join them, assuring me it was all fine with the diplomat, and in any case she'd never know.

Jil was unfortunately the most unreliable person I have ever met, although she was constantly resolving to do better and writing all her appointments on her hand in ballpoint pen so she wouldn't forget them. But it was a terrible personal flaw for someone with her politics, which were not quite separatist but at least mistrustful. She was always getting into debates with the men on the staff and lining up all the women to support her. Then she'd fail to show up for the urgent staff meeting she'd persuaded us to call, appearing only after it was over to demand a rediscussion and revote. She once arrived twenty-four hours late to a dinner party and then was surprised that no one offered to set her a plate. Typically, Jil ended up spending most of the march weekend not at the diplomat's apartment at all but rather somewhere in Virginia where her on-again-off-again girlfriend was ensconced, so they could fight in private. I didn't have a girlfriend, and my best friend was a man, so I stayed by myself in the diplomat's Watergate-style apartment complex way the hell out in Chevy Chase, where I had to face down the doorman, who sat behind a huge fortress-like desk and gave me the hairy eyeball, as though he'd just been perusing my FBI file, every time I went in or out.

When I had worked at *Sister Courage*, I couldn't help envying *GCN* its downtown office, its weekly publishing schedule, its paid staff, and its justified margins, despite their obvious explanation: patriarchy. Naturally a male publication had access to resources for fancy typesetting and frequent publication that we women could not even dream of. So in exchange for joining up and reaping the advantage of it all, I had vowed to use my position to preach the beautiful word of feminism to the unenlightened and to make sure that women got some benefit too, for a change. Or, that's what I would tell myself after I'd had dinner with my former *Sister Courage* pals or read a book by Andrea Dworkin and suddenly felt the need to rationalize the fact that I was hanging around with men day and night.

Not that the *GCN* men thought of themselves as working for a male publication. The way they saw it, there had been an abundance, if not, some whispered, an excess of women involved in the paper right from the start. It was one of the things Richard was proudest of, the fact that *GCN* had always been, as he described it, co-ed.

"Can't you say co-sexual or co-gender or something?" I said crankily, quite aware that these words were even more obnoxious than *co-ed*. "This isn't college. And anyway, why were only the girls called *co-eds?*"

Even the FagRaggers, who were by definition men only, took themselves quite seriously as feminists, and when they weren't publishing Charley Shively's "Act of Revolution" essay series, the most famous of which was "Cocksucking as an Act of Revolution," they were publishing manifestos about being feminist gay men and debates about what this meant. Were not gay men *men*, with all the privileges of their gender, and if so how could they get rid of them?

Actually, I'd figured out the solution to that problem during a conversation with Clover Chango, a radical faery given to diaphanous scarves, elflocks, spontaneous performance artistry, and the frequent consumption of raw garlic for the maintenance of good health, as well as a sometime FagRagger, during the intervals when he wasn't feuding with them: wear a dress. Even if I were wandering a deserted parking garage unable to find my car in the middle of the night in a neighborhood where the residents locked themselves inside their houses and never came out, and in that dark and fearsome place he suddenly appeared, rushing toward me, I would still never be frightened of a person who looked like Clover. There's no need to get a nice dress. Clover's were *schmattes* like the ones my mother wore to clean the house. And don't bother doing anything out of the ordinary about your facial hair.

The spectacle of gay men agonizing together about whether they were feminist enough may seem laughable now, looking back from the distant vantage point of our present era full of gay Republicans in gorgeous suits running around Washington advocating capitalism, war, and the criminalization of abortion. But in my opinion it was and is quite right for radical gay men and feminists to see their cause as one and the same. As Gregg and Harry would have said, "We're all girls together—even the *deeks*" (their special, fake-French pronunciation of "dykes").

My feminist crusade began to feel even more superfluous as I met the many other women who worked and volunteered at the paper; there were enough, in fact, to form the short-lived but notorious *GCN* women's basketball team. It flourished after Roberta Stone, *GCN* board president, broke up with her girlfriend and had only two-day-a-week child-care responsibilities for their son. Every Wednesday night she was at The Saints, asking anyone who caught her eye to dance, telling her, "I think you're very attractive, and I'd like to sleep with you." The lesbians were so shy and so astonished by Roberta's direct approach that it worked every time. "I'm not looking for love," she would have to admonish them.

Roberta had learned her bold cruising approach from gay men, although with them it is much more refined and subtle, with most conversation beside the point. The most interesting illustration of this I know is in an article *GCN* once ran about deaf gay people, in which the deaf men said they had no trouble picking up hearing men in bars, since they could easily achieve this through eye contact and body language. But finding

of sign language is to be unaccepting of

Reaching Out to Deaf Gays

By Chris Guilfoy

(l to r) Jim Sullivan, Nancy Becker, Kim Schive, Sam Feliciano

---

relationships was more difficult, as the hearing men had no patience for communication challenges. The lesbians had just the opposite experience. We eat communication challenges for breakfast. It's crossing what I used to think of as the sex barrier that is daunting, even though it often turns out not to be a barrier at all but only a little unevenness in the pavement, which trips you up only if you're really clumsy.

Even though Roberta is only five feet tall and in no way athletic, she became the basketball team's star player, and back at the office the group dynamics grew even more complicated than usual, as Roberta had affairs with the ad manager and various volunteers on both offense and defense. I avoid sports, so never got involved in the team, although both Roberta and I remember going out on a sort of a date during that period. Each of us believes she was rejected by the other.

The barrier was high between us, with her so suave and sexy—of course I knew her reputation—and me such a geek; so nothing happened between us until many years later, during a completely different time in our lives. Her best friend Bob Andrews had just died of AIDS, and her father was in the hospital. She had just broken up with her girlfriend, and they were trying to sell their apartment, since neither of them could afford to keep it by herself, so Roberta didn't know where she would live. She and I were having dinner together, and she said, "I can't even take a vacation this summer, I have no one to go with."

"I'll go with you," I said. Bob had been my friend, too, and as it happened I had also broken up with my girlfriend, although my parents were healthy, *keynehore*, and I had a secure rental. Things between us progressed from there.

But my point is that she learned from gay men. As did I. I failed to convert even one of them to feminism—they didn't need me for that, although Richard tells me I taught him to say "abortion-rights" instead of "prochoice"—but they welcomed me as an ally and became my friends and mentors, and I found myself saying words like *doll* and *fabulous* and waving my arms around and going out dancing with them on nights other than Wednesday. Richard dragged me to every gay bar in Boston, even to Playland and Over Harry's in the Combat Zone, where the clientele couldn't exactly dance with us—they could barely stagger from table to bar and back. I wore a pair of shrink-to-fit Levi's 501 jeans with a button fly, sometimes with the bottom button undone, although the effect was negligible, since I of course have no basket, nor any desire for one. It was a gesture of solidarity.

In other words, I went native. It wasn't what I'd expected when I first walked into the *GCN* office, but it was probably the best thing that ever happened to me.

Planning for the March on Washington had begun during the winter of 1979, at a big national conference in Philadelphia, with hundreds of delegates from all kinds of places and organizations—the Salsa/Soul Sisters from New York City, a contingent of tall men in pointy-toed boots and ten-gallon hats from Houston, and enough people from towns like Norman, Oklahoma, to form a Hinterlands Caucus. Richard, Eric Rofes, Dee Michel, and I were *GCN*'s delegation. Dee used to volunteer at the paper doing this and that and was a diligent if occasionally contrarian attender of meetings. Whenever he turned up, he and I would inevitably be wearing the same clothes, so we had a bond of taste. For example, if I was wearing my red flannel shirt with the cowboy motif, army surplus khakis, and Birkenstock sandals, so was Dee, down to the same style of sandal, only his shirt might be blue. A few years later, he took a bookbinding course—he had various esoteric interests—and for his final project he bound the first ten years of *GCN*s into huge lavender volumes, many of which are stacked next to me on my desk at this very moment. I've had them for several years on long-term loan from the Boston GLBT History Project, so every time I see Libby Bouvier, who founded the project, she says, "Don't forget to return our books, now." I reassure her that I refer to them every day, and I won't abscond with them. But I wish I could. Each volume has a special bookplate on the inside cover that says,

Bound by hand by
Dee Michel
for the

Gay Community News

on the occasion
of our
10th Birthday
June, 1983

In Philadelphia we had signed up for home hospitality, i.e., sleeping on the floor, so once we got to the city, I was dropped off by myself at a local lesbian's house, while Richard, Eric, and Dee continued on together to the Philly gay bookstore, Giovanni's Room, whose owner had offered to put them up. My hostess turned out to be a minister in the gay Metropolitan Community Church. She was wearing a big leather cross around her neck when she opened the door, and I worried that she would want to discuss religion, but since I had arrived fairly late, we didn't have time to talk for too long before I spread out my sleeping bag. Then, another guest showed up. She snuggled up next to me and told me she would be representing Lesbian Feminist Liberation. I was impressed. LFL had been one of the earliest lesbian organizations to come out of the women's movement in the late sixties; I had read their pamphlets. After we had lain side by side for a while chatting in the dark she reached over and pulled me to her, and I had to roll away to a different part of the floor and pretend to be asleep. In the morning she shunned me at breakfast, understandably I guess. But I thought that as feminists we should have been able to go back to our original friendly footing, so later, after we'd gotten settled in the conference

Conference co-chairs Dr. Walter Lear and Mariana Hernandez

Some delegates ponder the future

Photo by Daniel Tsang

Photo by Harry Eberlin

Plans Move Ahead for October March on Washington

PHILADELPHIA — Over 300 gay men and lesbians from throughout the country met here on Feb. 24-25 to discuss a proposed gay march on Washington, DC. Coming from as far away as

conference itself the ratio of men to women was 2:1 and there was a strong Third World presence.

To March or Not to March

The first major agenda item that the delegates discussed was

did not support a march during this year. Several delegates from Texas spoke of the need for more time to do local organizing before putting their energies into a national focus. Alice Schrader of

hall, I broke away from my little delegation of Richard, Eric, and Dee and went over to chat with her. She hissed back angrily, "I saw *what* you came in with." I didn't see her after that, so maybe she decided not to stay for the entire weekend; clearly she didn't have the right attitude for planning a co-ed, I mean, co-gender event. Years later I heard that she had gone on to found an extremely effective bug extermination business in Manhattan.

The conference itself was a contentious yet blindingly formal event, run according to Robert's Rules of Order, at which a surprising number of delegates seemed to be adept, at least enough to be constantly jumping up and yelling "Call the question! Call the question!" The meetings were chaired alternately by a man and a woman—both of them well-intentioned sociologists, who had probably felt that their most useful contribution to the movement might well be their experience as veterans of bitter academic disputes over tenure-track appointments and office allotments. They nevertheless found themselves in over their heads with this political crowd, and after the conference ended were never heard from again. At *GCN* we'd never run a meeting according to Robert's Rules or anyone else's, so mostly our group just watched the proceedings in awe.

A sizeable percentage of the delegates had apparently come to the conference expressly to squelch the march, which they feared would either be poorly attended or attended en masse by the wrong sorts of people, who would give all of us a bad name with their usual antics and bad wigs, focusing unwanted attention on the quieter kind of gay person. Or maybe that wasn't it, maybe they did want a march, but only on the condition of passing their own particular motions and amendments, friendly and unfriendly. At the last possible moment a majority voted in favor, and everybody cheered and hugged one another, and Eric immediately volunteered to be on the organizing committee, which astonished me, since this meant that for the entire next year he would be dealing with motions and amendments—although out of the four of us he had been the one who had most quickly caught on to the rules and begun raising his hand and making objections and such. Actually, Eric was prescient in understanding that organizing for the march would result, for the first time, in a national network of gay activists, who would know one another and have worked together and had one-night stands and doomed cross-country affairs and tragic break-ups. Until the march, most gay activists' attitudes were more parochial: "Who needs a national movement? We've got enough trouble at home."

GCN put together a special guide to the march, with articles about its history and significance, a program of the weekend's events, and maps of Washington. We ordered a press-run of 10,000, huge by our standards, assured by an excited guy who'd answered the phone in the march office that the organizers had recruited a brigade of volunteers whose sole task would be to help us distribute our special edition to the marchers, who, we hoped, would be so grateful for the information in it that they would immediately subscribe. On the weekend of the march, Richard, Jil, and I drove to Washington in a rented U-Haul truck crammed with the bundles of newspapers. The two of them appointed me navigator, and Richard marveled, as I got us lost time and again, "You always go the wrong way, but you always seem so sure of yourself." Tempers frayed as we wandered further and further into the suburban wilderness, our store of chocolate bars and peanut butter sandwiches exhausted and the needle on the gas gauge dropping lower and lower. At least I can't be blamed for getting the truck wedged under the gas station canopy at a service area on the Jersey Turnpike. In the end it took four guys to extricate the truck, one in the driver's seat and the others running around it yelling and pointing in different directions.

FREE   FREE

GayCommunityNews

Vol. 7, No. 12A   (617) 426-4469   © GCN, 1979   October 14, 1979

EXTRA   EXTRA   EXTRA

GUIDE TO THE MARCH

Lesbians and Gay Men Gather for National March

WASHINGTON, D.C. — The largest demonstration of lesbians and gay men in this city's history is expected to march down Pennsylvania Avenue on Sunday, October 14, as gay people and their supporters unite from across the nation to call for "an end to all social, economic, judicial, and legal oppression of lesbian and gay people."

The National March on Washington for Lesbian and Gay Rights, organized by a coalition of activists in all fifty states, is focused on five specific demands: 1: Repeal all anti-lesbian/gay laws; 2: Pass a comprehensive lesbian/gay rights bill in Congress; 3: Issue a presidential executive order banning discrimination based on sexual orientation in the Federal Government, the military and federally-contracted private employment; 4: End discrimination in lesbian mother and gay father custody cases; 5: Protect lesbian and gay youth from any laws which are used to discriminate against, oppress and/or harass them in their homes, schools, jobs and social environments.

Joyce Hunter, co-coordinator of the National March Office, told GCN, "We definitely expect people to be here from every part of the country. Planes are coming from Alaska and Hawaii, a group of lesbians has been bicycling to the March from the West Coast since June, and trains and buses will be converging on Washington from throughout the continental U.S. Lesbians and gay men are coming from Mexico and Canada, as well as parts of Europe, Africa and Australia. We expect this march to be a powerful call to end discrimination against lesbians and gay people in the U.S. and throughout the world."

While the largest concentration of March participation will undoubtedly be from the Mid-Atlantic and Northeastern states, strong contingents are expected from Florida, Texas, California, Ohio, Michigan, Washington, New Mexico and Oklahoma. A large contingent of Third World lesbians and gay men is expected to be present in the march formed as part of the National Third World Lesbian/Gay Conference, convening in Washington, DC this same weekend. Special contingents of gay youth, the physically challenged, and older gays are also planned.

Organizing the March

Organizing for the March on Washington began last autumn when a group of lesbians and gay men met in Minneapolis to discuss the possibility of marking the tenth anniversary of the historic Stonewall Rebellion with a massive national action focused on Washington, DC. While attempting to plan the structure and priorities of the march organization, the coalition met with unresolvable disputes, reportedly focused on the politics of the march and issues of sexism. In October 1978, the ad hoc committee officially disbanded.

Harvey Milk, the late San Francisco Supervisor, had agreed to continue attempts to form a march organizing committee. After Milk was assassinated in November, members of the San Francisco gay community, along with activists in Philadelphia and New York, issued a call for a national meeting to discuss the proposed march. The meeting, which occured in February at the Quaker Meeting House in downtown Philadelphia, was attended by over 300 lesbians and gay men and was marked by strong Third World participation and leadership. While the meeting was attended primarily by East Coast activists and was only ½ women, delegations were present from many areas, including California, the Northwest, Ohio, Texas, New England, and Louisiana. The three day conference, marked by much political debate, voted to issue a call for the march in October 1979 and planned the basic structure and demands of the March.

Throughout the spring of this year, lesbian and gay activists throughout the country debated the proposed march and began to plan outreach and publicity on a local level. A national office was opened in New York City and the process of fundraising began. Major national organizations, including the National Gay Task Force, Gay Rights National Lobby, and Dignity, issued statements that fell considerably short of endorsing the march and which questioned, among other things, the timing of the march, the
Continued on Page 4

Special Announcement

The organizers of the National March on Washington for Lesbian and Gay Rights have announced that the network of activists who came together to plan and carry out this march will continue to work together to plan a national meeting of lesbian and gay activists from throughout the country to discuss the direction which their newly-formed organization, the National Committee for Lesbian and Gay Rights, will take. The meeting will probably be scheduled in early 1980 and will be publicized in the lesbian, gay, and women's press.

3rd World Gays Convene National Conference

WASHINGTON, DC — The first national conference of third world lesbians and gay men is being held this weekend at the Harambee House in Washington, DC. Sponsored by the National Coalition of Black Gays, the five-day conference will include workshops, plenary sessions, cultural events, dances, a gospel session, and keynote addresses by black lesbian poet Audre Lorde, and Washington DC Mayor Marion Barry.

Darlene Arrington, co-chairperson of the National Coalition of Black Gays Board of Directors told GCN, "We are trying to recognize all elements of our community at this conference. Participation by anyone is welcome and there are specific workshops for non-third world

people." Workshops scheduled to be held include "Third World Lesbians and Autonomy," "Gay American Indian Information," "The Role of the Homosexual in the Black Family," "Sexual Revolution and Social Revolution: Focus on Cuba," "Lesbian & Gay Asian American Research," "Third World on the Outside, Non-Third World on the Inside: Coconuts & Oreos," "Surviving in Rural and Isolated Areas," "A Look at Racism and Sexism by the Non-Third World Lesbian and Gay Community: Where Do We Go From Here?"

Registration for the conference begins Thursday night at 6 p.m. The registration fee is $15, students may pay $5. On Thursday evening the conference will host An Evening of Culture, featuring

musicians, poets, and dancers, at the Harambee House at 9 p.m. The Friday conference schedule includes ethnic caucuses, gender caucuses, three series of workshops, plenary sessions, and an address by Mayor Marion Barry at 8 p.m. That evening, the conference will host a Nightlife Disco at Democritus International, 16 & R St. NW. The disco will be open until 5 a.m. and the admission fee is $3 for conference participants, $4 for non-conference participants.

On Saturday the conference will include regional caucuses, ethnic gender caucuses, as well as workshop and plenary sessions. At 6:45 a panel discussion will be held to discuss the role of third world participants in the March on Washington. At the 8 p.m. general
Continued on Page 4

National Lobbying Effort Planned for Monday

WASHINGTON, DC — On Monday, October 15, lesbians and gay men from throughout the nation will meet with their elected officials and lobby for support of the National Gay Rights Bill and for the March on Washington demands.

Organized by the March on Washington Lobbying Committee in conjunction with the National Gay Task Force, National Coalition of Black Gays, and Gay Rights National Lobby, the day has been planned as a way for senators and congresspeople to hear from their

gay constituency. Paul Boneberg, co-chair of the Lobbying Committee told GCN, "It's important for anyone who can stay in Washington on Monday to arrange to lobby their legislators. People from rural and conservative areas especially need to be here to show their representatives in Washington that they have a responsibility to the lesbian and gay men who are a part of their constituency."

Special Interest lobbying is also being arranged for groups of people who wish to meet with a

particular department or bureau. The National Coalition of Gay Health Workers will be meeting with officials in their area of concern to cite specific cases of oppression among health workers.

People interested in lobbying their legislators should call the Lobbying Committee any time throughout the weekend at 789-1070 and set up an appointment with their senator or congresspeople. Lobbying training sessions will meet Monday morning.

INSIDE:

March Route, Schedules, Events, Map, General Information, and Much, Much More . . .

When we finally found Washington, our first destination was the march office. We had been instructed to drop off our newspapers there to be picked up by the squad of volunteers who would distribute them around the greater Washington area. But when we made our triumphant entrance, expecting to be welcomed as the heroic bearers of essential supplies, like the mushers who raced the diphtheria serum from Anchorage to Nome, the harried march staff claimed to have heard neither of us nor of any of our contacts and ordered us to leave their office immediately and remove our newspapers, which we had begun unloading from the truck onto every inch of empty floor space. They even claimed they'd never heard of Eric, despite the fact that over the past year he had risen through the ranks to become one of the main march coordinators. All they would tell us was that we could probably get rid of a few bundles at bars. They gave us a handy bar map they'd printed up for out-of-town visitors—although we preferred to use our own, included in the special edition, since we had such an abundance of them.

We drove to a few of the recommended bars. Of course, it was impossible to park the truck, so Jil would drive around and around the block while Richard and I went inside. In the middle of the afternoon, they were dark, echoing spaces, empty except for maybe a couple of guys drinking at the bar, colored lights flashing over a deserted dance floor. After shouted conversations over pounding disco music a few managers agreed to take a bundle or two of papers, but most said they didn't want to carry anything "political." "Never mind," said Richard. "We'll hand the rest out at the march."

The special issue aside, it was an amazing weekend. Everywhere except the place I was staying, with its FBI-agent doorman, was swarming with gay people—the highway rest stops on the trip down, the city streets, the drugstore, the Smithsonian, the restaurants, the buses. When you boarded Washington's surreal automated subway, every passenger on it seemed to be headed toward the march, hauling signs and balloons. The doors would slide open, and a crowd of people would rush on. Then a shriek and in the middle of the car two women hugging and crying—long-lost high school classmates.

"You too?"

"You too?"

Rubbing each other's crewcuts. "Ha, ha! Your hair!"

"Your hair!"

Richard and I ran into his friend Kenny Rabb, who had ridden down to Washington from New York on the train. Before Kenny had moved to New York to go to law school he had worked in Boston as a projectionist in the gay porno theater and taken news photos for *GCN*. He said the atmosphere on the train had been a lot like that we'd experienced on the Washington subways, or maybe on the beach in Provincetown in July—only more so, with everyone talking across the aisles and bouncing from seat to seat and sharing drinks and sandwiches and blasting the latest disco song, "We Are Family," on portable radios. Pairs of gay men, including Kenny and a very attractive man he had met, bunched up at the ends of the cars as they waited their turn to push into the little Amtrak WCs together. The conductors could barely make their way through it all and yelled at everyone to sit down, but relented after a while as they found themselves much admired for their uniforms, mustaches, and hard, round hats. Complete strangers had bonded for life by the end of the ride.

Kenny introduced us to his trick, along with a couple of other new friends. Since Richard and I had been on our way to lunch, we now all continued on together, with me, as so often, the only lesbian in a troop of gay men. In Boston this was usually fine, and if I were treated in any way out of the ordinary it was as an especially delightful guest; but our new companions had traveled all the way from San Francisco, where suddenly in the late seventies so many gay men were popping up everywhere that Castro Street had become a kind of perpetual gay pride parade, or at least a perpetual pride of gay men parading, with no shirts, since by then the gym thing was starting up also. They paused occasionally for S&M—Stand and Model. And if you wanted to watch it all happening, you could sit in a sun-dappled gay bar with big windows facing right onto the street, so that any passing stranger could glance in and see for himself right away what kind of place it was. Yet the windows remained intact. What a contrast to our boarded-up Sporters back in Boston, or Buddies in the basement, or the Saints with its secret address and alternative afternoon identity.

I realized Kenny's new friends were unaccustomed to eating lunch with a lesbian, in addition to being distracted by Kenny, and once they had flashed their friendly western smiles at me, they didn't quite register my presence. It was strangely relaxing to be a disengaged observer nodding my head once in a while rather than having to blurt out a response or opinion every minute, as I did with my *GCN* friends.

The San Franciscans had worked together as aides to the martyred gay city supervisor Harvey Milk. Every demonstration seems to take on its own particular theme or spirit, although not necessarily the one the organizers have planned, and Harvey was everywhere at the 1979 march. What I liked about him was that he had not been an A-list sort of gay man. He wasn't a doctor or a lawyer or fabulously rich, he was more of a hippie drop-out. Before getting involved in politics he had run a camera store on Castro Street, just for a job; he wasn't a photographer. People started hanging out there with him, and it became his campaign head-quarters. After a while, he wasn't selling much film. He was a middle-aged Jew whose boyfriends were generally younger than he was and Latin. He was charismatic and funny and politically savvy, and gay people all over the country had been incredibly proud to have him representing us, even if it was as an official in a city where we'd never live.

Harvey and the mayor of San Francisco, George Moscone, were shot to death by Harvey's fellow city supervisor, Dan White, in November 1978. Right before the murders, White had handed in his resignation to Moscone, saying he couldn't live on his supervisor's salary. Instantly he had regrets and asked Moscone to reinstate him. Moscone refused, and White, an ex-cop, returned to City Hall with a gun. At the *GCN* office, we'd gotten the call about the assassination before it had been reported on the TV or radio or in the newspapers. So there was a brief moment when we didn't have to believe it, when it might have been some sort of wildly exaggerated rumor. Soon of course it was on the news and in the papers, and our phones were ringing off the hook: gay people were marching in the streets in San Francisco. They were marching in Boston. We rushed down to the corner to march with them. White was arrested immediately, and then for months, it seemed, the trial dragged on. Dan White's lawyer argued that his client was deranged when he fired the shots, driven out of his mind by the stress of working with commies and queers like Moscone and Milk, which was further aggravated by a constant diet of junk food—the infamous Twinkie Defense. The verdict came down at the end of May 1979, right before gay pride month: Dan White got seven years. The early, mournful vigils turned to riots in San Francisco.

GCN editorialized (as written by Richard and me) against the death penalty but also against the prison sentence: "There is no verdict that could have been handed down under our present systems of justice and of punishment that could satisfy us," we wrote. If Harvey had been straight, they would have locked up White and thrown away the key.

Generally I'm a pacifist, but like a lot of people I was secretly thrilled by the San Francisco riots. So-called pansies overturned fourteen police cars. They went nuts in the streets and smashed the windows at City Hall. All that gym muscle was not just for show. The Castro Street Clone look took on a fearsome new meaning—suddenly gay men were scary. Don't mess with him, man, he's a big *fag.* It was Stonewall all over again. Everywhere at the March on Washington, people who weren't pacifists were wearing "No Apologies" T-shirts, with a picture of a San Francisco police car in flames.

Others had made signs quoting, more or less, a tape recording Harvey had made to be played in case of his death. Maybe that sounds paranoid, but he knew that the murder of an openly gay politician would not be an enormous surprise to anyone. He had received death threats constantly. The signs said, "If a bullet should enter my brain let that bullet smash through every closet door in the nation." The image disturbed me. Forgive me for being grotesque, but the bullet enters Harvey's brain, exits, smashes through the closet door—and what? Injures or god forbid kills the person cowering inside? Okay, I understand what he meant: You have to come out. If it's anger and fear that motivate you, so be it.

Harvey would have loved the March on Washington. It was even bigger than the anti-Briggs campaign. This was people coming out not one by one but by the thousands, in front of TV cameras, in the nation's capital everywhere you went, including during lunch at a Vietnamese restaurant in Georgetown, where my companions were loudly debating Harvey's legacy. Was he a radical? Was he just another politician who would eventually have sold us out, or had perhaps already done so before he died? I wondered if he had supported lesbians, or if he'd been more like his oblivious friends, sitting with us eating spring rolls and noodles.

Kenny's Amtrak trick, Cleve Jones, went on to become a well-known AIDS activist in the 1980s; he was all over the news for organizing mourners into sewing bees to create the AIDS memorial quilt, which eventually included among its thousands of panels the one for Bob Andrews that I photographed at the quilt display on the Mall at the *second* gay march on Washington in 1987. (I also took a picture of the panel for Roy Cohn: "Bully. Coward. Victim.") That was the march where New York ACT UP showed up en masse, all of them looking fabulous with their cropped hair and new-style sideburns and humpy gym bodies—the women, too! They carried posters with a creepy pink and green day-glo picture of Ronald Reagan that had a stamp, AIDSGATE, across the bottom, because Reagan as president never even said the word *AIDS*, which had become a huge political scandal. Or should have. ACT UP blew everybody's mind. We all wanted to become part of it, and we went home and started our own little ACT-UPs—in Boston, we had both ACT UP and Mass Act Out, both doing ACT UP kinds of things, like staging a die-in at the Cathedral of the Holy Cross.

But all that was beyond what anyone could have imagined back at the first march in 1979. It would have sounded like science fiction, like what the *New York Times* originally called GRID, which sounds like something out of one of those futuristic Christian novels, where everyone but the sinners whose sin has become manifest as Gay Related Immune Deficiency gets sucked up into heaven by the Rapture. Oh, and the Jews—they don't go either.

The day of the march dawned damp and gray. The *GCN* contingent had instructions to gather on a particular street corner, in front of a forbidding gray stone building, the CIA or the Supreme Court or something like that, with an outsized staircase leading up to it, like just about every building in certain parts of Washington. When I arrived, a small group was already there, holding up our banner, some of them the old familiar staff, but some none of us had ever seen before: they turned out to be our national writers, whom we had previously met only on the telephone. Or, quaintly, through typed letters.

Somehow, the *GCN* special edition arrived at the march also, and Richard announced that we were all to take a bundle and to hand out papers to anyone who would take one. Some of us started doing this immediately, giving *GCN*s to the members of the other contingents who were assembling around us. I had plenty of experience at this, since we always had *something* to give out at demonstrations—back issues, subscription flyers. The best way to get people to take your stuff was to catch their eye and to say, "Free gay newspaper?" and then to thrust it into their hand before they could respond. "Free" is important. "Free gay newspaper? Free gay newspaper?"

When it was finally our turn to step off, because as with any long march the marshals kept us waiting forever on the sidelines until they identified the exact, appropriate place for our contingent, which was between something like the Imperial Court of Cleveland, a group of lesser drag queens feting their elected Emperor and Empress with loud music and extravagant dance, and the Unitarian Universalist Welcoming Congregation Committee of Three Corners, Vermont. Eventually the Unitarians, half a dozen white-haired ladies in Keds and plastic rain hats, were elbowed aside by the FagRaggers, whom no one else would allow to march beside them with their PORNOGRAPHY, PROSTITUTION, PROMISCUITY, PEDERASTY! banner. Typically, they made distributing our special issues much more difficult, by intervening every time we said "Free gay newspaper" and sticking the spectator, who was by rights *our* customer, with the old *FagRag* with the pen-and-ink penis drawing on the cover. Fortunately, we were all long gone, at least a half a block farther down the parade route, before the recipient could decipher the drawing and hand the *FagRag* back. The FagRaggers also liked to make up their own, unapproved responses to the chants:

> *What do we want?*
> *Gay Rights!*
> *What do we want?*
> *Gay Riots!*
> *What do we want?*
> *Straight trade!*

The dykes on bikes and the lesbians of color led the march. All manner of glamorous drag queens, from the Statue of Liberty to Barbra Streisand, some with five-o'clock shadows, some speeding by on roller skates, cavorted among the marchers—having their photographs taken now with the parents of gays, now with the lesbian moms, now with the bar floats blasting disco music, the clean and sober gays, the Catholics, Protestants, Jews, Pagans, Seventh-day Adventists, college students, lesbian drummers, S&M people sweating stoically in their leather outfits, the teachers, the elders waving from their bus, the youth blowing raspberries at the spectators, the Democrats, the Workers World Party, the square dancers,

the bowling leagues, the stamp collectors, the marching bands and ba-
ton twirlers and choruses singing Broadway favorites. I can't possibly list
every kind of group that marched, even that first time, when you didn't see
some of the kinds of groups that fill gay pride marches now, such as high
school gay/straight alliances, gay and lesbian police, workplace support
groups of bank tellers and computer programmers and healthcare provid-
ers, all with large colorful banners donated by their sponsoring companies,
Log Cabin Republicans, and not one or two lone ethnic individuals but entire elaborate floats gotten up by groups like gay Pakistanis in sari drag.

It was drizzling when we arrived at the rally site, where the copies of
GCN began to fly from our hands, people taking them not because they
were excellent reading material but because they made useful cushions on
the damp ground.

"Free gay newspaper?" I offered.

Richard tapped me on the back. "Amy," he said. "You and I will be
doing this in Hell."

I should have been feeling exhilarated, and part of me was—loving everyone around me, all those brave souls risking ridicule and loss of whatever was important to them—parents, children, friends, apartment, job—to
show themselves here. But I was also hungry, cold, and suddenly lonely.
Everywhere I looked people were kissing and hugging and proudly holding hands—and I wondered, Where is my girlfriend? Who are my friends?
What happened to Jil Clark, my erstwhile lesbian traveling companion? Am
I a lesbian if my best friend is a man? Maybe it was nothing more than low
blood sugar and lack of sleep, but I didn't see where I fit into the vast happy
crowd. Richard pulled at me. "Sit down, Aim. Where are you going?" He
wanted to hear every word of every speech on this historic occasion, even
though there was an endless succession of them. The important speakers
were seated on the stage, but the lesser ones must have been lined up somewhere out back, because they kept appearing one after another, sporadically
audible depending on the wind direction and level of feedback, while the
number of people onstage didn't seem to be diminishing.

"I'll be back," I said. "I want to look around."

He consulted his program. "But Allen Ginsberg is up next!"

I shook my head and made my way to the top of a small rise. A bearded
man had stepped up to the mike, but he wasn't Allen Ginsberg. Gay people
surrounded me in every direction, stretching so far that I could not see

where the crowd ended. Onstage the bearded man was replaced by a lesbian folksinger with long red hair. Unaccompanied, she began to sing a song that I happen to know so well that it is lodged in the most primitive cells in my brain, because my mother sang it as a lullaby. It is also, as everyone knows but my mother, a gay male anthem. "Somewhere . . ." sang Holly Near. All around me people were standing up and linking arms. Below me I could see Richard towering over the rest of the staff. ". . . over the rainbow." A strange man took my hand and drew me into the line of swaying people. Everyone knew all the words, and together we belted them out in the drizzle: "Skies are blue."

All day, during every step of the march and every hour of the rally, everyone in our contingent had been frantically handing out *GCN*s, yet after it was all over, Richard and I returned to the truck to find the piles of papers apparently undiminished. "How can that be?" I said. "We tried so hard." Before he and I could go home, we had committed ourselves to one last errand: distributing the rest of the newspapers.

"Come on," said Richard. "Let's get this over with."

Our idea was to finish the tour of Washington's gay bars and gathering places that we'd started when we first arrived and to give as many papers as we could to anyone who would take them. But Richard made a sudden turn down an alley that I couldn't find on our map. "No, no, not here," I said. "You're going the wrong way."

Richard pulled up next to a small vacant lot with a phone booth in the middle of it. "Do you have to make a call?" I asked. Even from the front seat of the truck I could see that the phone was unusable. It had no receiver, and one side of the booth had been kicked in. Richard climbed down from the driver's seat.

"Aim, come help me with this, would you?"

Bundle by bundle, he began taking our newspapers out of the truck and throwing them into the telephone booth.

"Richard! I'm sure this is trespassing! It's littering! What if somebody comes?"

"They won't," he said. "Here." He passed me a bundle.

When we'd completely filled the telephone booth we began piling the papers around the outside of it. As we'd contracted, the truck was clean and empty when we returned it to the rental office. Richard said never to tell anyone, but I'm glad to get this off my chest after all these years.

100,000 March in Washington

By Rick Hillegas

WASHINGTON, DC — More than 100,000 people marched and rallied in Washington on Sun., Oct. 14, demanding "an end to all social, economic, judicial, and legal oppression of Lesbian and Gay people." More than a year's planning culminated in this first national gay rights demonstration.

At noon, starting at the Mall opposite the Smithsonian, the marchers proceeded down Pennsylvania Avenue and 17th Street to the rally grounds in front of the Washington Monument. The larger contingents came from New York state, Massachusetts, California, and Texas. Contingents, each numbering from a couple score to several hundred, represented Birmingham, Boston, Chicago, Cleveland, Detroit, Houston, Indianapolis, Los Angeles, Madison, Milwaukee, New York, St. Louis, San Fran-cisco, and Washington. Smaller contingents and people with handsigns represented smaller cities such as Clarksville, KY, Lansing, MI, Pawtucket, RI, and Watertown, NY.

Groups that marched included the Illinois Gay Task Force, Gay Farm Workers, Abortion Rights Movement of Women's Libera-tion, Gertrude Stein Democratic Club, Gays and Lesbians of AFL-CIO, Lesbian Herstory Archives, Gay Dads, Lambda (NH) Gay Youth, Broome County (NY) Gay Alliance, National Lawyers Guild, and Gay Caucus of Members of the American Psychiatric Association. Campus groups marched repre-senting, among others, the University of Iowa, State University of New York, Sarah Lawrence College, Stanford, and Harvard-Radcliffe. Several religious groups marched, including Gay Mormons United, Affirmation United Methodists, Dignity, Integrity, Metropolitan Community Church, and Jewish Gays. Individuals car-ried handsigns such as Gay Envi-ronmental Chemists, Country Faggot, and I Know You Know.

Two predominantly straight or-ganizations, the New York Revolu-tionary Socialist League (RSL) and the Workers World Party, brought large contingents. Each carried several megaphones and scores of printed banners. While assembling before the march, RSL members chanted "Gay Rights are Gay Riots" until march organizers warned them that the Houston Conference which had planned the march had overwhelmingly voted for a non-violent demonstration and proscribed violent chants. March marshalls reported that during the march RSL members tried to provoke the police with homophobic taunts such as, "I bet you want to suck on this, don't you?" The Workers World Party distributed literature featuring homophobic pictures and cartoons.

Spectators along the march route were mostly friendly, though three tear gas canisters landed among the rearmost marchers and two men carrying "Repent or Perish" and "Jesus Saves From Hell" signs confronted marchers opposite the White House. Outside the Rayburn House Office Build-ing some 100 Christians prayed that gay people would repent.

The rally started at 2:00, even though half the marchers had not yet entered the rally grounds. Standing closely packed in the muddy grass for four hours, the crowd stretched from 17th Street back to the Washington Monument.

Comic Robin Tyler and march Transportation Office coordinator Ray Hill emceed the rally. Speakers included National Gay Task Force co-director Lucia Valeska, Nation-al Organization of Women (NOW) president Eleanor Smeal, NOW vice-president Arlie Scott, San Francisco City Supervisor Harry Britt, co-sponsors of the national gay rights bill Representatives Ted Weiss (D-NY) and Phillip Burton (D-CA), and poets Allen Ginsberg and Audre Lord. Entertainers included Meg Christian, Holly Near, Tom Robinson, Blackberri, and Gotham.

Three themes dominated the

Continued on Page 9

John Tobin

I'm sorry now that it didn't occur to me to buy a march T-shirt or even a button to remember it by. I lack the socio-historical, shopping-and-collecting gene. Whatever is happening, being involved in *GCN*, going to ACT UP demonstrations—it's simply what I'm doing, day to day, minute to minute. Only later do I realize that it actually had a particular mood or shape or significance. Some things I've done in my life because I'm a particular, idiosyncratic person, but other things, it turns out, I've done or thought or felt along with millions of others as part of some vast cultural tropism.

What I mean is, I don't always correctly distinguish news from the chaos of everyday life. But even I knew instantly that the march was headline news. It was unique, unprecedented, and big. The speakers at the rally had announced crowd estimates all day, as we poured onto the Mall: there were 90,000 of us, 100,000, 125,000, which was easy to believe after our encounters with one another all over Washington, not to mention the amount of time it had taken for everyone to complete the march route and arrive at the rally. Then, the police estimated 25,000. Around the country, newspapers snubbed the event. Our contingent arrived back in Boston exhausted and euphoric, only to find a crummy one-graf note buried in the middle of the *Globe*, when we'd been looking for big pictures of ourselves splashed all over the front page. Our weekend in the capital seemed to have taken place in some invisible dimension, our vast numbers and marching feet and lifted voices only a strange ripple in the air, a momentary "did you hear something?" My landlord David Peterson and Raymond Hopkins on the second floor were so infuriated that they did what they always did in such situations: call a meeting. Raymond served dinner to everyone who showed up, and over one of his casseroles and a nice green salad they founded the Lesbian and Gay Media Advocates. They wrote letters, they met with editors, they picketed, they yelled at the *Globe*, and while they were at it, any other medium that slighted gay news. In other words, except for *GCN*, which we couldn't even give away, all of them.

8

The Swan Princes

In the late seventies the *New York Times* stringer in Boston was a reporter named Dudley Clendinen. Richard, always on the alert for anything having to do with the *Times*, used to call him regularly with leads for gay stories. This was more in the nature of harassment than of helpfulness, because there was no way in the world that the *Times*—or the *Boston Globe*, or the *National Enquirer*, for that matter, with its focus on space aliens—would have considered anything we did fit to print. The *Times* stylebook forbade the use of even the word *gay* until the 1999 edition, insisting on *homosexual* except when it was too long to cram into a headline or when a reference to a group such as the National Gay (now Gay and Lesbian) Task Force was unavoidable. The stylebook did not tell reporters how to handle references to *FagRag*. It didn't have to.

At *GCN*, we could never have come up with such terminology regulations. We were still trying to determine the politics of punctuation. When I joined the staff the gay male writers told me they hoped I would not be like a previous lesbian editor who they claimed had forbidden them to use semicolons, saying their long, unfurling sentences were "too male." I have no problem with semicolons; but we all have our hobbyhorses. I once had a showdown with a reviewer who insisted on using the word "centrality" rather than taking my edit, "importance." I told him "centrality" sounded pompous.

"What's wrong with sounding pompous?" he said.

We had more arguments about how to refer to ourselves than about any other issue in the history of the paper, including evergreens like the morality of intergenerational sex, and how to require Mike Riegle, our office manager, to process payments made with credit cards, which he believed to be a capitalist plot and rejected on principle. In 1973 when the paper was founded, each word in our name *Gay Community News* had contained within it an entire political statement:

Gay: The early gay organizations of the 1950s and 1960s had used the most arcane kinds of references in their names so their nature would be clear only to initiates: the Mattachine Society, the Daughters of Bilitis. Even organizations founded later often had names that were obscure, quaint, or bland: the Lambda Legal Defense and Education Fund; the Homophile Community Health Service; the Human Rights Campaign Fund.

Community: Although it may seem too obvious for comment now, the claim that gays were a class of people with a common culture and interests—rather than isolated cases of perversion—was revolutionary, the heart of the gay liberation movement.

News: Not only that, but the things we did together and as individuals were noteworthy, interesting, and had an audience.

By far the most contentious word in our name was *gay*; the least, *community*. *News* came into dispute only later in the paper's history, as bans like the *New York Times*'s were dropped, and it became possible to find information about ourselves in the mainstream media. Covering breaking news became less essential for *GCN*, and in fact without the staff and technological resources of papers like the *Times*, *GCN* often got out the facts less efficiently than they did. This caused a growing identity crisis at *GCN* throughout the late eighties, as the paper lost its audience and sense of mission. Although *GCN* eventually attempted a format that focused on political discussion and cultural coverage, the unresolved question, If we are not a newspaper what are we? was one of the factors—as well as a finally hopeless financial situation exacerbated by possible fraud—that led to the end of *GCN* as a weekly newspaper in 1991 (although it continued publishing quarterly until 1999).

But at any point in *GCN*'s history, the easiest way to start an argument would have been to walk into the office and say, "I'm gay." Oh yeah? Lesbians, especially we younger ones, felt we were not included in *gay*, and insisted on *lesbian* for ourselves and *lesbians and gay men* for the aggregate. When some new volunteer, coming to her first membership meeting and unaware of the uproar the suggestion would cause, would raise the topic of changing the name of the paper to *Lesbian and Gay Community News*—which happened regularly—there was always someone to argue that this was divisive, and it was better to unite as *gay people* and to avoid redesigning the masthead. To me, *gay* used to sound old fashioned and prefeminist. Nowadays, I like it. It's old school, the badge of a long-timer. But I remember my hesitancy to admit to anyone that when I had come out to my mother, I had retreated at the last minute and said, "I'm gay," instead of "I'm a lesbian." *Lesbian* sounded so graphic, almost obscene. Among ourselves, we said *dyke*. The men called each other *fag*, but rarely have I, as an outsider to this category, felt comfortable calling a gay man a fag. Whenever we used *dyke* or *fag* in a *GCN* headline, as in "Dykes and Fags Oppose Nukes," illustrated with a photo of a perfectly androgynous protester, we caught hell. An older man once cornered me at a benefit for the paper to berate me about it, refusing to let it go no matter how much I explained that we were trying to transform the old insults into words of power. As the list we had started by insisting on *lesbian and gay* got longer and longer—as in *lesbian, gay, bisexual, transgender, intersex, and questioning*—some of us wished we could just say *queer*. That was the word I grew up with, the one I knew the definition of viscerally, the word on the playground: "Ahh, ya queer!" *Queer Community News*. We all liked it, but we knew it would never happen. It was the final frontier.

In 1992, Dudley Clendinen came out, on his employer's op-ed page, no less. Richard and I discussed it briefly, with a kind of triumphant bitterness: "Remember Dudley?" Next we heard that, like everyone else one met at the time, Dudley was writing a book about the history of the gay movement. This was after the 1993 *LGBT* march on Washington, the one that was hijacked by a cult of people who believed that if only gay men and lesbians could serve openly in the military all our troubles would be over. Heading up the gay marches of the seventies and eighties had been contingents of lesbians and people of color, to demonstrate the diversity of our movement, but the 1993 march had been led by an honor guard *gepootzt* from head to toe in the dress uniforms of the various military services— well, we'd seen that before, but these people didn't lip-sync or twirl batons or do anything particularly entertaining. They marched in step, eyes front, while the rest of us crowded behind them, waving our signs and cheering and jumping out of line whenever we spotted an old friend or a hot dog vendor or a glamorous drag queen with whom we could have our picture taken. A few contingents of radical faery veterans had sewn themselves gowns of camouflage cloth trimmed in shocking-pink grosgrain, but they were shunned by the marching vets. The whole campaign was a big mistake, in my opinion, but then I still have the War Resisters T-shirt and peace symbol earrings I wore in high school, and I still wear them. The march did have the positive result of causing a unique, fleeting moment in literary history, as editors at several large publishing conglomerates, overcome perhaps by the barrage of attractive young people in uniforms, became briefly convinced that books about the history of the gay moment, Dudley's among them, were going to start selling like miracle diets.

I have no idea who told him I would be a good source of information about Boston, but naturally I was flattered to get his call and discover I was a historical personage. I was also totally curious to meet him, the symbol to us for so many years of the implacable *Times*. I was genuinely disappointed that our interview was not a success. The main thing Dudley wanted to talk about was the Anita Bryant demonstration, which had happened, or rather not happened, on September 1, 1978, right before my time at the paper, although of course I'd heard stories.

Does anyone remember Anita Bryant, or has her name become one of those that sounds vaguely familiar for some unknown reason? The former Little Miss Terrific, Miss Oklahoma, Christian chanteuse, and Florida orange juice mascot ran a successful campaign in 1977 to repeal the Dade County, Florida, gay rights ordinance, pointing out that "if gays are granted rights, next we'll have to give rights to prostitutes and to people who sleep with *St. Bernards* and to nail biters." Triumphant after the Florida victory, she decided to take her organization, Save Our Children, national. "As a mother," she told her followers, "I know that homosexuals cannot biologically reproduce children; therefore, they must recruit our children." Was it all our marching that gave rise to this ironically military language? Howard Phillips, a mad-dog conservative who was running for the U.S. Senate in Massachusetts, immediately invited her to speak at a campaign rally. Anita's marriage fell apart sometime in the 1980s, she lost the juice gig, and eventually fell into well-deserved obscurity. However, her malign influence continued until 1998, when the Dade County gay

EXTRA — EXTRA — EXTRA

FREE

gay community news

Vol. 6 No. 6A   ©GCN, 1978   (617) 426-4469   September 1. 1978

Coalition Formed to Protest Visit

Anita Bryant to Appear in Boston

BOSTON — Nearly two hundred members of the lesbian and gay communities, along with non-gay supporters, met Thursday, Sept. 24 at Boston's Old West Church to decide on an appropriate response to the scheduled appearance of Anita Bryant on Sept. 1 at a fundraiser for Howard Phillips' bid for the United States Senate. Those present at the meeting formed the September 1 Coalition, an ad-hoc group that has assumed responsibility for all aspects of the demonstrations.

Phillips has invited Bryant to sing and speak at a "pro-life, pro-family rally" at Hynes Auditorium in the Prudential Center. Phillips expressed his "particular pride" in having Bryant hold a rally on his behalf. "Mine is the first political candidacy she has campaigned actively for," Phillips said. Phillips characterized Bryant as a leader "is a number of moral fights in which pro-life is emphasized."

The participants at the September 1 Coalition meeting expressed a desire to show support for all those human rights threatened by Bryant's so-called "pro-life" stance. The participants

and Am Tivka were in attendance.

After a lengthy debate, a collective decision was made to have an on-the-site demonstration. Resolutions were also passed supporting women's right to choice, an invitation to religious leaders to speak, and permission for supporting groups to raise funds at the demonstration.

At later committee meetings, an outreach committee was formed to contact concerned groups throughout New England, a publicity campaign was begun to contact persons in the Boston area, and the details of the demonstration were settled.

The demonstration itself will begin at Copley Square, Friday at 6 p.m. From Copley Square there will be a march to Hynes Auditorium where the demonstration will continue for the duration of Bryant's appearance. The participants will then march to a location yet to be announced for entertainment and dispersal.

Volunteers are still needed for various aspects of the protest. There will be an opportunity for representatives of concerned organizations to speak

Anita Bryant

are asked to gather at 5 p.m. Friday in Copley Square on the steps of Trinity Church, where Dave Drolet, John Mitzel and Kathy Travers will conduct an

3 p.m. only.

The Coalition is planning to offer housing and child care services needing or offering housing should

---

rights ordinance was finally reinstated—a déjà-vu repeal initiative was defeated in Miami as recently as 2002. She is credited with being a harbinger of the politically engaged religious right.

Bryant was a reprehensible bigot, but she was also ridiculous—sentimental, hypocritical, bad hairdo, apt to break into song. It was so unfortunate she was a woman. The lesbians at *GCN* felt obliged to argue that the grotesque caricatures of Anita that the art director published week after week were misogynist. But of all people to have to consider a sister! Even if in only the most general kind of way. It was a classic dilemma: As I had heard it posed at *Sister Courage*, Who is our ally, Jacqueline Kennedy, or Jacqueline Kennedy's garbage man? Did feminism demand that we empathize with and even respect the slights, the subservience to men, the oppressiveness of traditional roles that Anita had undoubtedly experienced in her life—even though her reaction to these experiences had not been to struggle against them but actually, as Miss Oklahoma, to celebrate them, and ultimately, as the leader of the Dade County fight, to codify them into law? A feminist would have had to be deluded—wouldn't she?—to consider all women her allies. The schisms even in the movement were legion—the lesbians vs. the straights, the separatists vs. the humanists, the Lesbian Sex Mafia vs. the Women against Violence and Pornography in the Media. The antagonists didn't consider one another sisters; in fact, the debates got so vicious that they didn't usually seem to consider one another quite human. Still from time to time, the question surfaced: Anita Bryant, Phyllis Schlafly, Jeane Kirkpatrick. It was particularly annoying that they made no pretense of practicing what they preached: they didn't stay home with their kids as they told everyone else to do. They went rampaging around the country, founding hideous yet successful political movements, acting mean and nasty whenever they felt like it, and giving interviews to the *New York Times.*

When it was announced that Anita Bryant would appear in Boston, a group of *GCN*ers began planning a major demonstration. It immediately bogged down in controversy. Some people in the community insisted that it would be a better tactic to ignore Anita. The bar managers jumped in with a call to boycott *GCN*—for lack of objectivity, rabble-rousing, existing, whatever. Fortunately, the boycott damaged the paper's income less than it might have, since the bars rarely paid their bills even when they did take out ads. Within *GCN*, a vicious argument broke out about whether or not to produce an extra edition calling on the community to demonstrate—the more practically minded reminding everyone that the event had already begun driving away our advertisers. The introduction of petty financial considerations into a political decision finally pushed the pro-extra faction, represented and consisting mostly of Eric, over the top, and Eric ended up having to produce the thing single-handedly. In the end, Anita cancelled her rally—because of the threat of the demonstration or because of the threat of being shunned, no one knew.

Dudley wanted to know who had organized the demonstration, what the point was of the boycott, why Anita backed out. I tried to be helpful, but I couldn't tell him much. Finally, he asked, "How was the controversy covered in the *Globe* and the other media?"

I was stunned. He must have known what a ridiculous, utterly pointless question this was. "Dudley!" I said. "You were there. Did *you* cover it?" Hardly.

The things that are missing are also history. *Nothing in this account makes any sense* if you don't understand how completely off the map we were—"here be really perverted, sinful, rebellious dragons." Dudley ap-

ISSN:0147-0728
VOL. 7, NO. 30
THE GAY WEEKLY 50¢
BIPAD: 65498
FEBRUARY 23, 1980

GayCommunity News

Cruising Opens Nationally

Appleby Found Guilty

Gay Men & S/M: Two Views

parently forgot that, or repressed it—maybe he should take it up with his shrink—and I know I should read his book, and I'd probably learn a lot, but I'm boycotting. At *GCN*, any time an openly gay person appeared in the back pages of mainstream newspapers, it was an automatic front-page story for us, especially if he or she had done something other than get arrested or die. We ran headlines when Tennessee Williams—the Glorious Bird, as Gore Vidal used to call him—drunk and singing, was mugged one night in Key West. And why not, a great American playwright of the twentieth century victimized in a common crime? But it didn't much interest anyone else. One of the muggers tried to kick Williams in the face but missed. Williams's friend told *GCN*, "It was then I started to think they were New York drama critics." As in all such stories, the final paragraph said police were investigating but had made no arrests. *GCN* reviewed every single book or film of gay or lesbian interest, which did not take up undue space even though we ran only 16 to 24 pages an issue. Even homophobic productions got a lot of attention. Week after week in 1980 we covered gay demonstrations against the film *Cruising*, which starred Al Pacino as a cop who pretends to be gay to catch your typical humpy gay serial killer. There was a little secret about those demonstrations, though: after each one, at least some of the picketers would sneak in to watch the movie. The chance to see gay bars and gay men onscreen, no matter how perversely depicted, was irresistible.

Recently a friend was telling me stories about an underground newspaper where she had worked in the mid-seventies. She said some of the people involved in it had clearly been social misfits—they looked funny, they didn't seem to have any friends. Her group had assumed these misfits were undercover police agents. But they were probably just gay. They probably ended up at *GCN*, where everyone was a misfit, and police agents, such as they were, came to us in a different form—like our local reporter David Brill, who never shut up about his pals down at headquarters. Undercover he was not, because there wasn't much point in being undercover at a gay newspaper—just walking in the door was the very definition of undercover.

My favorite storybook when I first learned to read included a tale about a girl with five brothers who had been turned into swans. I'm going to get the plot all wrong, but it doesn't matter. She had to knit magic sweaters for them, which would turn them back into humans. The enchanted swans came for their sweaters, flapping down around her in a whir of white feathers and squawking, and she threw the sweaters over them, and the flapping calmed, and feathers floated to the ground and stuck in her hair, and suddenly the girl was surrounded by five handsome princes, ready to carry her away from the promontory next to the crashing sea where she had been imprisoned while doing her knitting. Or rather, she was surrounded by four and three-quarter handsome princes. When the swans arrived she had yet to finish the last sweater. The brother who wore it ended up with a swan's wing instead of an arm. The other brothers were kind enough to pretend not to notice, and he was forever after the girl's favorite brother, whose wing, she thought, was quite beautiful.

As a child I identified wildly with the girl—her isolation and solitary occupation; her large, weird family. Later I saw certain parallels to *GCN*— the girl's life among the princes, her shame at blowing her impossible deadline. But eventually I identified mostly with the swans: our beautiful wings, when we were left them, treated as bizarre deformities or at best invisible; our mysterious swan adventures frightening or disgusting, but in any case of no use or interest to the people among whom we walked; our humanity blurred by the shadow of our ever-disconcerting—and perhaps even deliberately chosen—experience of flight.

[1.] Tenth Anniversary Celebration, June 1983. Photo by Marie Favorito.
From left, back row: Ken Sjonnesen, David Peterson, unidentified (half-obscured by hand with balloon), Bruce McLay, Satya Littlebear, Mike Riegle, Richard Burns, Larry Goldsmith, George Dimsey, David Morris, Kevin Cathcart, Jeremy Grainger, Dee Michel; *third row:* Urvashi Vaid, Will (Harry) Seng, Gregg Howe, unidentified, Sherry Edwards, Denise Sudell, Amy Hoffman, Nancy Walker, Neil Miller, Nancy Wechsler, Jil Clark; *second row:* Lisa (Hershey) Hirschkopf, Cindy Patton, Tom Huth, Bob Andrews (wearing his *GCN* fire shirt), Cindy Rizzo; *front row:* Raymond Hopkins, Sue Hyde, Eric Rofes, Maida Tilchen.

[2.] "Donna Louise Puts Out the Paper," cartoon by Roberta Stone, circa 1979.

[3.] *GCN* staff and volunteers at the March on Washington for Lesbian and Gay Rights, October 1979. Photo by Susan Fleischmann.
From left: Maida Tilchen, Mike Riegle (hidden by Maida, wearing cap), Neuma Crandall, Amy Hoffman, Richard Burns, Eric Peterson, Cindy Rizzo, Kim Mohr, Rob Schmieder (hidden by Kim, with glasses and beard), Rick Hillegas, Gordon Gottlieb.

[4.] David Brill, by J. Berndt.

[5.] Amy Hoffman (left) and Urvashi Vaid, with the *GCN* banner at the Pentagon, U.S. Out of El Salvador protest, 1981. Photo by Susan Fleischmann.

[6.] "Your first orgy," by Jennifer Camper, 1980.
To avoid embarrassing me, Jennifer named the character on the right "Jane,"
rather than "Amy."

[7.] Nancy Walker and Mike Riegle. Photo by L. Severance.
The occasion for the photograph is the artwork hanging on the
wall, a unicorn etched on leather and framed in wood and copper
by Mike's prison penpal, Bobbie Lee White, a great fan of Nancy's
Odyssey of a Unicorn column.

[8.] "The Bells Ring Gay," Arlington Street Church gay pride banner. Photo by Susan Fleischmann.

[9.] Amy Hoffman, speaking at the Arlington Street Church after
the *GCN* fire, July 1982. Photo by Ellen Shub.

[10.] Boston gay pride march, June 1980. Photo by Susan Fleischmann. Richard Burns and Amy Hoffman yak in the second row.

9

The Death of David Brill

Whereas David P. Brill was an outstanding journalist, firmly committed to the principle that democracy requires a well-informed electorate; and

Whereas in pursuit of these principles, David Brill pioneered in helping the gay and lesbian community understand how government and politics function in Massachusetts; and

Whereas David Brill also pioneered in reporting on relations between the gay and lesbian community and law enforcement authorities in a manner which did more to improve these relations than has the work of any other individual or organization in Massachusetts;

Therefore be it resolved that we express our sense of loss at this death, and our deepest sympathy to his family and friends.

Resolution offered in the Massachusetts House of Rrepresentatives, November 1979

When I called my mother the morning after David Brill died, she said, "You'll get over it, sweetheart." Like he was a lost pencil. My mother is not cold-hearted, or inarticulate. But unfortunately, Brill, like all my friends and associates, and for that matter anything having to do with my daily life, simply had no reality for either of my parents.

The entire time Brill worked at *GCN*—in other words, from the founding of the paper until the day he died—he lived with his family in Winthrop, a peninsular suburb next to Logan Airport, whose citizens like to feel their enclave is tranquil and uncitified, although really it's just hard to get to from anyplace else. A few weeks after the funeral, Brill's mother and sister turned up at the *GCN* office. Richard showed them around: these are David's desk and telephone; this is our display on the walls of back issues, he's got stories in almost all of them; these are the bullet holes in our front window (okay, maybe Richard refrained from showing them those). As they left, they thanked him tearfully. "We had no idea about any of this," they said. Apparently, Brill hadn't been entirely real to them either. Not that their belated tour would help, because as anyone around the office might have told them: Dolls, you don't know the *half* of it. Their David, son and brother, took classes at the University of Massachusetts and went to temple on *shabbes*. His hobbies were writing and playing the piano. Whereas our Brill was constantly rushing from his friends on the police force to those in the state legislature to his underworld sources to his tricks, whom he'd sometimes bring up to the office and onto the green couch with the batting that leaked from its cushions and stuck to your pants—well, he could hardly have taken them home to Winthrop.

"I don't want my parents to wait until I'm dead to get to know me," I cried melodramatically after the Brill family left. Then and there I entered my parents' names into the *GCN* subscription list. Previously, I had shown them only the masthead, which I had clipped out and mailed to them after my first week of work at the paper. My father had responded with a letter: "Your name looks good in print," he wrote. "I still can't get used to the publication but that's my problem. I hope you can learn and gain experience and then get a paying job." Actually, *it was* a paying job, but apparently not so you'd notice—when I sent my parents the subscription, we'd just gotten a raise to $100 per week. They wrote me more letters after they read their first issue. Unfortunately, it was the one with the cover drawing of the lady with the boots and the whip and the wicked grin—not what I would have planned for them, but stopping the subscription before it had even started seemed cowardly, and in any case I had no reason to think the next week's cover would be better; in the way of these things it would likely be worse. In addition to the cover story on lesbian sadomasochism, the issue included the first installment of a medical advice column by Ron Vachon from the Fenway Community Health Center, the gay clinic. I was very pleased I'd finally succeeded in persuading him to write it. He had chosen the topic "Anal Pleasure and Health."

"This is not how I was brought up," my father wrote while my mother wanted to know why I had abandoned the Jewish people, whom God had commanded saying, "Be fruitful and multiply," an obligation that she and my father, with their six children, had taken with unusual seriousness for Jews of their class and generation, but that she erroneously assumed was not a lesbianic prerogative. It seemed too complicated to enlighten her,

especially since I personally had no intention of messing around with turkey basters, flash-frozen sperm, fertility drugs, or Chinese adoptions. The
contents of *GCN* were never again mentioned between my parents and
me, and I used to picture each issue dropping sadly through mail slot to
the floor, and my mother taking the smallest possible corner of the envelope between two fingers and disposing of it in the trash before my youngest brother and sister, still living at home, could discover it and started
asking questions.

When I got home from layout on the awful night of Brill's death, my
roommates were long asleep. Alone in the silent kitchen—away from the
ringing telephone, and the crying people, and the suddenly meaningless
race to put out the week's issue—I thought I'd be able to figure out what
I felt about Brill. I sat at the table with a cup of tea. Not exactly crying.
Not exactly not.

The truth is, Brill wasn't real to me either.

I can easily recall his shrill voice, and the dropped *r*'s and twisted *a*'s of
his Boston accent. He was always excitable, outraged. But I can't remember a word he said, unless you count his phone salutation: "Brill here!"
(To bug him, Jil Clark had begun answering her line, "Jil here!") With his
dark little mustache, his briefcase, his trench coat, plaid shirts, polyester
pants, and paunch, he liked to be thought of as a man of mystery—one of
which was why a twenty-four-year-old queen would dress that way. When
the obits came out, I was shocked to discover I was two years older than
he was. He had started writing for the paper when he was nineteen. I had
thought he was, like, forty.

It wasn't only his appearance that had given me that impression. It was
his disdain. David Brill was a genius surrounded by idiots like me, who
could barely see over the wall into the fields where his genius played. He
did not take assignments or submit to editing. He wrote what he wanted,
when he wanted, about the beat he'd carved out for himself: crime, cops,
the city bureaucracy, the state legislature—in other words, the establishment, the belly of the beast, with which I and most of the rest of the staff
tried to have as little to do as possible, on principle. The paradox of Brill
was that his best accomplishments lay in his defense of gay people against
the depredations of the police even as he fawned on the police—at least
those who were his sources. The others, his enemies, he pursued relent-

lessly. He filed complaints. He made a fuss. He even succeeded in having a few disciplined for beating up gay prostitutes, which at that time was generally seen as a perk of the job. Cops fascinated him, perhaps even more than those whom they'd failed to help or actively victimized—although a lot of those "Brill here!" phone calls at the office were from the victims, for whom he acted as a sympathetic referral service and one-man police review board.

Still, there were the rumors: that Brill had betrayed, that he had named names. By the late seventies, the police rarely raided gay bars and house parties. Instead, they concentrated on cruising areas, after-hours clubs, and periodic—often election-year—round-ups of vast, fantastic conspiracies of gay pornographers and child molesters. Brill, some said, helped in such frame-ups. No more than a youth himself, maybe he believed he was striking a blow against exploitation—who knows what his own experience had been, or what scars he carried? Brill believed in law enforcement: the law should protect gay people equally with others, as it should be used against them when they transgressed. Ultimately, his was the gay conservative point of view. He did not question the underlying fairness of the laws themselves, nor the evenhandedness of the system that created and enforced them.

There was actually a long-running *GCN* dispute, completely ignored by Brill, about whether his beat should be covered at all, whether it could really be said to constitute essential gay news. Wasn't the real story the evolution of our own, alternative institutions? Wouldn't these lead to true social change in the long run? Fed up with our coverage of such distractions as state and national elections, Clover Chango wrote a letter to the editor castigating us: "Alternative/radical political analysis and cultural expression are frequently overshadowed by coverage of reformist politics. Needless to say, I am thoroughly disappointed with the inadequate coverage of the Festival of Lesbian and Gay Culture (especially when I see all this conservative stuff taking priority)." He himself had organized the ill-attended fest, which perhaps undermines his argument—but his letter represents a typical complaint. Brill, who'd stuck with the paper longer than any of us, stayed above that and all frays, well aware that if he simply persisted, we and our complaints and controversies would vanish and be ground into dust. He assumed he could outlast any annoyance we created.

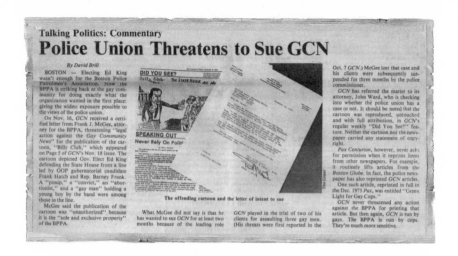

Talking Politics: Commentary

Police Union Threatens to Sue GCN

By David Brill

BOSTON — Electing Ed King wasn't enough for the Boston Police Patrolmen's Association. Now the BPPA is striking back at the gay community for doing exactly what the organization wanted in the first place: giving the widest exposure possible to the views of the police union.

On Nov. 16, GCN received a certified letter from Frank J. McGee, attorney for the BPPA, threatening "legal action against the Gay Community News" for the publication of the cartoon, "Billy Club," which appeared on Page 5 of GCN's Nov. 18 issue. The cartoon depicted Gov. Elect Ed King defending the State House from a line led by GOP gubernatorial candidate Frank Hatch and Rep. Barney Frank. A "pimp," a "convict," an "abortionist," and a "gay man" holding a young boy by the hand were among those in the line.

McGee said the publication of the cartoon was "unauthorized" because it is the "sole and exclusive property" of the BPPA.

What McGee did not say is that he has wanted to sue GCN for at least two months because of the leading role

GCN played in the trial of two of his clients for assaulting three gay men. (His threats were first reported in the

Oct. 7 GCN.) McGee lost that case and his clients were subsequently suspended for three months by the police commissioner.

GCN has referred the matter to its attorney, John Ward, who is checking into whether the police union has a case or not. It should be noted that the cartoon was reproduced, untouched and with full attribution, in GCN's regular weekly "Did You See?" feature. Neither the cartoon nor the newspaper carried any statement of copyright.

Pax Centurion, however, never asks for permission when it reprints items from other newspapers. For example, it routinely lifts articles from the Boston Globe. In fact, the police newspaper has also reprinted GCN articles.

One such article, reprinted in full in the Dec. 1975 Pax, was entitled "Green Light for Gay Cops."

GCN never threatened any action against the BPPA for printing that article. But then again, GCN is run by gays. The BPPA is run by cops. They're much more sensitive.

The offending cartoon and the letter of intent to sue

With a precocious understanding of the power of publicity, even in a medium as woo-woo as *GCN*, Brill methodically built the paper, whose name most of the politicians and police he covered could barely bring themselves to pronounce, into a personal power base. On Friday afternoons, when the printer delivered the paper to the office, he could be found sitting at his desk behind a pile of newspapers and envelopes, barraging every remotely relevant person with tearsheets of his articles, making sure his subjects and his sources knew he was watching them.

Brill did things like read the police union newsletter, a wildly right-wing rag called the *Pax Centurion*, and he was always digging up neanderthalish racist and homophobic statements from it, which he would then reprint in *GCN* in the Did You See . . . ? column. Which of course you hadn't, because who else read that stuff? The policemen were furious to see their articles constantly bumping up against Brill's latest scoop about drag queens who'd been beaten up by cops while hustling on the Block or guys who'd been gay-bashed in the Fenway Victory Gardens, and once the *Pax* actually threatened to sue *GCN* for violating their copyright. We were thrilled, since we knew, even if they didn't, what little *pishers*—as my grandmother and Brill's would have said—we were. The threat resulted in some exciting posturing by their lawyer and ours, John Ward, a radical faery who kept a lucky crystal tucked into the vest pocket of his impeccable suit and who once had to make a complete opening argument with his hands clasped behind his back, when he suddenly realized he had forgotten to remove the glitter nail polish he had applied during a weekend faery circle. Eventually all the lawyers got bored, and the lawsuit was dropped.

David Brill died on Thursday afternoon, November 15, 1979. Thursday is the key. Our Brill, the Brill we knew, would never have killed himself on a Thursday, the day the paper went to press. Without a note and on a Thursday—these acts seemed so out of character that I suppose he successfully maintained his air of mystery to the end, and beyond. NO FUCKING WAY, Eric Rofes e-mailed me, when I asked him whether he had concluded, after all these years, that Brill had killed himself. A friend of Brill's, as much as Brill could have been said to have friends, Eric said Brill always warned him, "If I die, and they say it was suicide, *don't believe it*." Brill talked about threats.

So the theory was that Brill had been forced or deceived into taking the cyanide that the autopsy tests found in his blood. "That would have been the perfect crime," Winthrop Police Chief David Rice, pokerfaced, told Neil Miller, who wrote Brill's obituary for the Boston weekly *Phoenix*. Our point exactly! The police investigators discovered that Brill, claiming to be a Winthrop High science teacher, had bought an insect extermination kit containing the cyanide earlier in the week. The store clerk described him and the clothes he had been wearing. A receipt was found in his pocket. The empty cyanide containers were found in his basement. QED. Case closed.

An assortment of David's friends and acquaintances, as well as *GCN* staff members like me and FagRaggers who believed Brill was basically a police spy but who couldn't resist a conspiracy theory, took out a full-page ad in *GCN* explaining our perspective:

> Most of us who have entered the arena of social activism have grappled with the labels ranging from naivete to paranoia. Yet, given the long history of death threats against David, is it paranoid for us now to be concerned? Given the overwhelming history of police and judicial collusion with all sorts of lesbian and gay oppression, should we not now be suspicious, not closely question "official" findings? Given the power, connections and expertise of the forces which are now only too relieved to hear David's pen lie silent, is it paranoid to expect that such forces would be quite capable of convincingly staging a suicide? We don't think so. We find it naïve *not* to question.

Even now, reading it, I can again start to wonder what really happened to David, alone at home, that Thursday afternoon. But no new evidence ever surfaced to contradict the police report. It all fits together, even if it doesn't make any sense.

We were just starting to lay out the paper when the phone rang. It seemed impossible: everyone had just seen Brill the night before, at a *GCN* benefit party at Buddies, a new bar. He didn't always attend such events, but he'd been at this one, big as life. When it was over, Eric and he had shared a cab, and Eric insists Brill was full of plans.

I don't remember who answered—it could even have been me. Normally, it would have been Richard. And he would have known what to say to whoever was on the other end, and he would have called those who needed to be called right away, and not called those who could wait—but Richard wasn't at layout that night. He was on Long Island with his family, at the funeral of his younger brother, Jamie. The week Brill died had not been a normal week. It had been a terrible week from the very beginning, when Jamie, far away on the West Coast, had gone out to celebrate with his roommates—he'd found a great job; he'd been looking since he'd graduated from college the previous spring. Early Monday morning, happy, high, exhausted, they'd all fallen into bed. Jamie didn't wake up.

There's a framed black-and-white photo of Jamie in Richard's apartment that I look at whenever I visit. Richard never refers to it, but it's always there. Jamie is tall, thin, leaning against a wall with his hands in the pockets of his overalls, a bandana on his head. He has shoulder-length hair, as Richard used to, although Richard's hair has been short now for years. In the photo, Jamie looks terribly like Richard, with Richard's cheekbones and his height and his eyes. Or is it that Richard has his brother's eyes, and carries Jamie with him?

What did I know about that kind of loss? While Richard was at home for the funeral I talked to him a million times a day on the phone, as always, babbling about this and that—the latest goings on at the paper, which relatives had shown up at his house. He had been kicked onto a new plane of existence, of grief, pain, and triviality. Somebody run out to the store, there's no cream for the coffee. It's chilly in here. Who's driving Nana to the cemetery? Because I was Richard's great friend, at *GCN* people kept asking me, "How's Richard?"

BIPAD: 65498

ISSN: 0147-0728

GayCommunityNews

VOL. 7, NO. 19 ■ THE GAY WEEKLY 50¢ DECEMBER 1, 1979

Select Commission Hears Immigration Concerns

David Brill: In Memoriam

"How's Richard?"

"Okay," I said. "I don't know."

They hesitated to call him themselves, because they didn't know what to say. "Say anything," I had decided.

When Brill died on Thursday, some of us were stunned and silent, and some began making phone calls all over town. I called Richard. At a certain point, the office phones started ringing back with people who wanted to make sure we'd heard, and I could have timed the velocity of the gay grapevine and come up with an equation: x (sensationalism of news) times y (number of people who know) equals z (time it takes for what goes around to come around). Eric came hurtling up the office stairs, and I caught him in my arms. His momentum nearly knocked me down. We held each other. I felt the heat of his body in the cold November night. He must have run all the way from his apartment wearing only his light blue sweater. I remember the sweater.

There's nothing in that week's paper about David Brill; it's all in the following issue. All we could bear to do was to slap the thing together and get out. We didn't have the technology to stop press, anyway, even to make a simple front-page box with a black border. Our cover image was lame, a publicity still from the Bette Midler movie *The Rose*. Bette plays a doomed rock star who does a lot of drugs, gives a few fabulous performances, and drops dead. Richard and I went to see it after he had come back from Jamie's funeral, and he started going to the movies to cry. We also went to see *Ordinary People*, which starred Mary Tyler Moore and Timothy Hutton, whom Richard said he longed to see without his shirt. We would buy sandwiches in Harvard Square and eat them in the theater, and by the time we had finished our dinner, the plot would have advanced to the climactic sad and desperate part, and we would each sit secretly crying in the dark, neither acknowledging the other, although handing each other tissues after the credits, as we climbed the raked aisle to the door.

In 1976, several years before his death, Brill had published the longest article he ever wrote for *GCN*, a reflection on suicide. He cited Sylvia Plath, whom he pointed out had been a fellow Winthropian. Expressing sympathy for gay people, especially gay youth, struggling with depression, he blamed the isolation caused by homophobia and class barriers for many suicides. He advocated coming out as a remedy, a step toward wholeness and authenticity—a step he himself was never fully able to take. In the end, his life must have become a tangle of live wires that he could not allow to touch, lest they spark a conflagration—home can't touch gay can't touch police can't touch tricks. No matter where he went, he was saddled with a secret life.

So in fact he wasn't totally real.

Or he was, but as the drag queens define "realness": where the performance is all there is. The mask that never slips, because it's no longer a mask. Brill strove for realness, but it was an impossible commitment.

Maybe "realness" explains Brill's vendetta against Elaine Noble: because she transcended it. Elected as the first open lesbian to hold office in Massachusetts, or just about anywhere else, in 1974, she was out in the state legislature—a body that had all the social sophistication of the Winthrop High School football team, complete with fist fights, all-night budget-negotiation beer blasts, and incidents of mooning. No matter, Elaine was out to her colleagues and her constituents, to the *Boston Globe* and no doubt to her mother. Initially an avid supporter, the disgruntled Brill published countless exposés and ad hominem attacks on Elaine's political dealings, her girlfriends, her real estate purchases, and whatever else he could dig up. To him, it all amounted in one way or another to a betrayal. She'd moved on, abandoning him and all the other gay working people who had given her her start, the class traitor Brill strove not to be.

If Elaine represented Brill's past and possible future, then Barney Frank was his present. Their relationship was more than that of reporter and source: both were Jewish, disheveled, fast-talking, smart, and pols to their very core, Barney actually the age that Brill appeared to be. Like Elaine, Barney was serving in the Massachusetts legislature, but he was so deeply in the closet it was hard to imagine him ever coming out—except, as with so many closeted people, everyone already knew. The gay men in the *GCN* office were always claiming to have run into him in one far-flung bar or another, outside his district. A straight friend of mine once brought up Barney's well-known secret to clinch her argument that the *Boston Globe* was not homophobic, asking me why, if they hated gays so much, the reporters didn't simply write what they knew about him. She maintained that their hesitance was not sourcing but respectful discretion.

Many people remember Barney as visibly broken up when he stood to speak at Brill's memorial service—a totally weird event in the way that all obsequies are weird, I've finally learned, and each uniquely. The funeral had taken place earlier in the week, for the family, so the memorial service was for Brill's friends and community. It was held at the Arlington Street Church, where the Unitarians rang their bells every June to the cheers of the gay pride marchers. I'd gone to innumerable community meetings and cultural events there, with choruses that sang old union songs, epic poets, one-act plays, tributes from absent celebrities read by the MC, and nuns from Central America. Since it was a Unitarian church it offered no hymnals or Bibles to flip through as the evening wore on, and the pews grew ever harder and higher, and the babies in their backpacks started crying, and onstage appeared the a capella singer of "Swing Low, Sweet Chariot." At Brill's service, one person after another went to the podium to eulogize him, at first people like Barney, who spoke with deep feeling and admiration of Brill's achievements and acts of kindness and quirks, but as the evening wore on, anyone who had the notion. Even the FagRaggers piled on, unable to resist the chance to offend the mourners by castigating Brill as a pathetic running dog of the establishment.

The service had begun with a recording of the theme from *Exodus*, I guess to represent Brill's Jewish heritage. I found this so personally humiliating I practically had to get up and leave right then. It's ridiculous to be memorialized with the theme from *Exodus*, it's not a *prayer*, for god's sake, or even religious. Even worse, hearing it reminded me that as a child I had thought it the most gorgeous music in the world, with its swelling minor chords and chauvinist lyrics. The grownups said it was *good for the Jews*. Maybe it was a Brill favorite, although I think it's more likely that it was the only Jewish piece whoever was put in charge of the music could come up with. At least it wasn't "The Dreidel Song."

Or "Love is Here and Now You're Gone," which is what Richard said we should have headlined the *GCN* editorial that he and I wrote after he came back from Jamie's funeral. He immediately realized that *GCN* had to make some sort of official statement, and called to ask me to meet him at the office. On a dark fall weekend afternoon, no one else around, the two of us worked uninterrupted on it for several hours. But it isn't really "love is here" at all. It's an inadequate little piece, which talks about *our* demand for an investigation—I loved getting to use the editorial *we*—but says nothing particularly personal or admiring about Brill's idiosyncratic style and accomplishments. When Richard and I were criticized for our insensitivity, I harshly defended what we'd written for exactly that reason. I claimed that we had represented Brill as he was—not that I had ever had even one extended conversation with him, nor quite understood what he was up to with all his running around and telephoning—without sentimentalizing him or glossing over his faults. That, I insisted—and even now would insist, if only we had managed it—was the most respectful way to memorialize the dead.

Brill may have feared he would become like Elaine Noble, but he was so young—for all his individuality still not fully formed—he might have become anything at all: corrupt or incorruptible, more arrogant or less. He might have continued to write or become an insomniac recluse, sitting up every night listening to a police scanner. Or he might have finished college, changed his clothes, found a husband, and run for city council. Anything.

"Life can be improved upon, you see," Brill had concluded his suicide article, "but death cannot."

10

An Army of Ex-Lovers

Urvashi used to complain about my ex-lovers. "Your *literary* girlfriends," she would say. "I am not *literary* enough for you." As usual, she had a point, sort of. I would have liked to have literary girlfriends, and even more to have been literary myself so as to attract them, but really it was only Andrea who qualified. She had written two entire novels, one of which had even been published.

To me, Andrea seemed to live on a higher plane. She once wrote that when she was growing up, she was always aware of the three things that distinguished her family: they were Jewish, they were immigrants, and their great-grandfather was a thinker so influential that his name has entered the English language as an adjective. She had no idea how many people belonged to each category. When I was growing up, I thought all old people had accents. I didn't know when or how I would acquire mine. But in Europe my relatives had been obscure schlemiels, not great genius-es of the twentieth century. On my bat mitzvah, a horde of my great-aunts and uncles, whom I didn't remember ever meeting before, had shown up to great acclaim, except from my grandmother, whose siblings and in-laws they were. She scorned her youngest brother, Louie, in particular, to the delight of my own younger brothers and sisters, muttering, "*Farshtupte kopf,*" stuffed head—but not with brains. The day after the celebration these relatives took me with them into the city for a nostalgic *shpatzir,* a stroll around the Lower East Side and then blintzes at Ratner's Dairy Restaurant. They spoke with their accents, they gazed up at the tenement fire escapes where they'd slept on stifling summer nights. Andrea also kept her eyes fixed above, on the higher, artistic plane, even if she was only taking a walk to the grocery store. Richard would say, "I ran into your friend Andrea. She was staring into space as usual. I had to get right up in her face to make her say hello."

Just the other night I found myself at a meeting with Andrea's friend Cindy Cohen, whom I had not seen for about a million years. It isn't so remarkable that I should have run into her, since Boston is simply not that big. Everyone comes back around eventually, and life feels like one significant coincidence after another. Cindy used to play the piano, although she probably no longer does, just as I no longer play the violin, but when we knew Andrea we played the piano and violin for her. Andrea would listen as we played and doodle picture after picture of us with a set of multicolored markers that she brought to our sessions for that purpose. She was tone-deaf and had no sense of rhythm whatsoever—which I already knew from trying to dance with her at the bar. She would nod her head behind the beat, then ahead of it, and her tin ear no doubt explains why she genuinely enjoyed our musical soirees. I liked the concept. The three of us together, *artistes* all. It was almost as good as being literary.

Cindy doesn't look much different all these years later. She has the same, sudden smile—nothing for a moment, as though she's considering, and then the sun comes out—and the same aura glowing faintly around her that used to halo all of Andrea's friends. I miss those auras. As I've gotten older, I rarely see them anymore. The people I meet seem less amazing, less likely to make me want to throw over my whole life, if that's what it takes to remain in their presence. Andrea's aura was always quite obvious, embodied in her long, kinky hair. In her book jacket photo, her hair fills most of the frame, and when I finally got close enough to her to bury my face in her hair, it gave me a rash, every time.

I had no doubt that this strange allergy was my body reminding me of Betsy. I was making a big mistake, and I knew it, but I couldn't *feel* it. You could have stuck me with pins. Insanely I was risking Betsy, whom I adored, who had her own bright halo. Betsy drove a pale yellow VW beetle with a bunch of weird smelling dried flowers, or maybe they were Chinese herbs, hanging from the mirror in a crocheted pouch, and at first we spent a lot of time hiding out and kissing in her car, even though things between us were instigated—I want to be clear about this—by

Betsy, who suggested one afternoon when I'd ridden by on my bicycle for a cup of tea, "Let's give each other massages."

Because I'd had a difficult day. At the *GCN* office, a male volunteer had called me a terrible name, one we had been experimenting with reclaiming as a term a strong, proud woman might use to refer to one of her favorite body parts. What had set him off was that I had been carrying my bicycle down the office stairs, and he had offered to help, and I had declined. I've never understood why he became so agitated about this; one theory I had was that he had misheard me and thought *I* had called *him* a terrible name.

Betsy and I went into her bedroom, and I lay face-down on her bed, and she said, "Relax," and I tensed all over, muscles poised for flight. I couldn't surrender to Betsy's thrilling massage because I didn't know what it was, heavy flirting or just something Betsy and her friends always did of an afternoon. And the reason the volunteer had called me a cunt and the mystery of the massage have more in common with each other than you might think: these ambiguities arose because all of us—volunteer, me, Betsy, friends—aimed to create nothing less than a new world with new social rules, where the arbitrary boundaries that define relationships and separate one human being from another would fade away like the bad-trip delusions of Patriarchy. Unfortunately leaving everyone writhing around and not knowing how to behave. Couldn't Betsy offer a simple massage without being misinterpreted by idiots like me or disloyal to Nancy Wechsler, her girlfriend? Anyway, shouldn't we have been smashing monogamy?

Another theory I had about the name-calling incident was that the volunteer experienced my refusal of help as an insult and thought I was implying that I scorned him and his puny male assistance—but really I feared that help at that unsteady moment would upset my balance, always precarious, and the two of us and the bicycle would end up in a heap at the bottom of the stairs. Ironically, later that very afternoon, I found myself in a situation similar to his: I couldn't figure out what it all meant. Was I being toyed with? *The medium is the message*, people said then. In my case, the medium was the massage. The massage was the message. Or maybe the massage was just a massage.

With lesbians interpretation is notoriously difficult. Roberta once invited a woman on what she thought was a date, but as the evening wore on she began to get the feeling that it might not be a date, and finally she demanded: "Is this a date?"

And the woman said, "I don't know."

The next day she called and said, "No, it was not a date!" This is not an uncommon experience, even now.

Knees still shaky after the massage, I left Betsy's house to discover my bicycle was gone. I had made the classic mistake of locking it to a random sidewalk obstruction, a short pole with a small knob on top, without examining it carefully. The thief had lifted my bike right over the knob, which still annoys me, because this method implies that he or she did not know how to disable the special lock, and had probably tried smashing it, ruining both bike and lock. I've been plagued all my adult life by incompetent thieves, like the junkies who broke into my apartment when I was in college and made off with a busted television and a packet of cat pills, and don't get me started on the people who take the car radio. I blamed myself about the bicycle, because I should have known better, but Betsy also felt responsible and gave me a ride home, which was when all the kissing in the Volkswagen began. After that, it took many months before Betsy could bring herself decisively to break with Nancy, who to this day gets a look in her eye when she sees me, as though she would like to call me a terrible name.

Betsy and Nancy both wrote for *GCN*; in fact, Nancy had introduced Betsy to it, something she perhaps came to regret. Nancy was one of the paper's most stalwart writers, sometimes toiling as the only feminist in the office, other times, as during my era, receiving a little more support— at least for her articles, although perhaps she would point out that her girlfriend did not leave her when she had only gay men to contend with. I believe it is Nancy who gets the credit for inventing the lead, "A small but spirited group of demonstrators . . . ," for occasions when only five or six people showed up, as well as the tactic of attributing to a friend among them a quote as to why, as a gay or lesbian person, he or she supported rent control/a woman's right to choose/U.S. out of El Salvador. The lead and quote were necessary to establish not simply newsworthiness but appropriateness for *GCN*, since there were two camps regarding the question of how far gay liberation should extend. The one that included Nancy and Betsy and me—and Andrea and Urvashi, for that matter, because we were all political allies even as our personal relationships grew more entangled—believed it was all connected, gender/race/class. The other camp wished *GCN* would cover a gay story once in a while, *gay*, get it, and while we were at it, quit saying *fag* when we meant *homosexual gentleman.*

Actually, I had observed Betsy Smith even before she came into the office and pulled a chair over to my desk to discuss an article she wanted to write. That was the difference between her and me: I'd *seen* everybody in town; she actually *knew* them. I had been sitting with Cynthia at the Boston Women's Music Festival, mostly absorbed in my own drama, but even so, out of the corner of my eye, I took note of Betsy, who stood out in the crowded balcony of Sanders Theater, with her group of laughing friends and her dark hair and dimples and blue-green eyes that can catch me by surprise even today, after thirty years. She was wearing a gray fedora hat like the ones my father used to wear to work when I was a child, but by 1978 men had of course stopped wearing hats to work, and they ended up in the sale bin at Oona's Nostalgic Clothing in Harvard Square, where lesbians bought them—in Betsy's case, to adorable effect. Across my desk, the woman I had observed at the concert was revealed as Betsy, hatless, explaining her plan to write an article based on interviews with the children of gay parents, who at that time were mostly toddlers, so the interviews would be quite challenging. Betsy looked at me with those eyes of hers and invited me home for tea. I would have fallen for her even without the massage, although without the massage, I would never have let on.

I was emboldened to send Betsy a Valentine's Day card, the first I had ever sent to anyone, not counting the ones we distributed to our classmates in elementary school, even those we didn't like, who pushed to the front of the line to play tetherball in the schoolyard. The card I sent Betsy had a picture of the Queen of Hearts, impassive in all her regalia. In accordance with holiday tradition, I signed it, "Your secret admirer."

Betsy was a nurse at Boston City Hospital, working nights, weekends, double shifts, and I of course worked at the paper all the time. After her evening shift she would pick me up at Thursday night layout, and we would eat dinner with Richard at the all-night restaurant in Copley Square before going back to her apartment to make love and smoke cigarettes until 3 a.m. We would show up at each other's apartments at odd hours—weekday afternoons or in the middle of the night. At the gay pride parade, instead of marching all the way to the end and then sitting on the Boston Common in the hot sun for hours listening to every last speaker at the rally, as Richard always insisted was necessary, Betsy pulled me out of the march on Charles Street. "Let's henna our hair!" she said, as we ran to catch the subway. It turned out to be a chore that had to be done naked, and afterward, in bed, I had a strange, ecstatic vision of Betsy's hands inside me creating an intricate palace—transparent, beautiful. Our dark hair glowed red for weeks.

But even though we were finally in a relationship, each of us remained independent, with other friends and commitments. As feminists this was our ideal, since it stands to reason that one person, no matter how multifaceted, cannot satisfy the numerous desires and interests of another. I had read *The Second Sex*, and then even more avidly the volumes of Simone de Beauvoir's autobiography, where she tells how, at one point, she and Jean-Paul Sartre lived without benefit of marriage on different floors of the same Paris apartment building. I admired their relationship more than any I'd ever heard of, especially since at that point I had never seen a photograph of the goblin-like Sartre, and I regretted that there were hardly any apartment buildings in Cambridge, let alone one with two simultaneous vacancies.

Instead there was Betsy's flat, where she lived there with her roommates, to whom she was devoted. One of them was the evil homewrecker Ellen, who had stolen my moon-goddess Cynthia from me, although when I found myself breaking bread with her at Betsy's kitchen table I never mentioned our previous connection and tried to pretend I had never heard of her before. I had heard a great joke about exactly this kind of situation—it was great simply because it was a joke about lesbians; in the new society we even had our own jokes!—that went, "There are really only ten lesbians in the world. It's all done with mirrors." Actually, it was a caption from a cartoon in *Christopher Street*, which we *GCN*ers used to disapprove of because it so blatantly aspired to be a gay *New Yorker*, yet with a more circumscribed territory. In those days a lesbian cartoon in the straight *New Yorker* was inconceivable—although by now you might think the *New Yorker* had aspired to be *Christopher Street* instead of the other way around. (Exhibit A: A drawing of a couple of men in their living room, one on the phone, saying, "No we're not going to the march this year. We're here, we're queer, we're used to it." A person could write a dissertation about the taming of the confrontational "Get used to it!" into the laconic "We're used to it," the usage of the word *queer*, the bourgeois comforts depicted in the well-dressed men's living room—but can *New Yorker* readers really recognize parodies of chants from the gay street actions of the 1980s? I find it hard to imagine, but then, I also used to have trouble believing that non-Jews took an interest in news from the Middle East.)

Nobody tells the mirror joke anymore, I suppose because it's become such a truism it's no longer funny. My friend Hanna, in her twenties, sniffs, "Dyke drama. I've had enough of that." I was not entirely distressed to see that Ellen was less appealing close up than she had seemed with Cynthia between us. She was going through an identity crisis and had begun dating men, instead of my girlfriend, one of whom, a hearty blonde guy who played the guitar often and badly, would also show up in the kitchen. Betsy and the other roommates grumbled about how much space he occupied, with his loud voice and beefy arms, and agreed that Ellen, as a lesbian, or former lesbian, should have had the tact to find someone more humble and retiring.

The roommates were nice to me, but they surrounded Betsy and took up all the empty spaces in her calendar, with special walks and talks and intimate breakfasts. When Betsy went away to Guatemala for a month to learn Spanish, the roommates gave me a ride to the airport for her home-coming, and they brought so many flowers and signs and cute little pres-ents that I, empty-handed, could not squeeze my way past them to greet her, and hung back, waiting to be noticed, which I finally was, it wasn't as terrible as that, and with lots of hugs and kisses; but despite Simone and Sartre and my feminist ideals, I wanted to come first.

We used to believe that lovers might come and go, but that friends would stick around forever. But we had drawn the wrong conclusion, fail-ing to take the long view. The mirror-magic of the lesbian community depends on friends becoming girlfriends and vice versa, and eventually all of them turning up at the kitchen table. Richard used to say, "You can't choose your family—and you can't choose your friends, either."

Andrea had been hanging around the office because she was between jobs and had begun writing for the paper, several really good essays about gay writers. Of James Baldwin she argued that critics had always under-appreciated his novels in relation to his essays, because it's in the novels where he really drops his hairpins. She also wrote a piece on Ann Bannon, whose series of 1950s lesbian pulps starring Beebo Brinker, a tragic butch despite or perhaps because of her kooky name, had been reprinted by Naiad Press. Even though younger lesbians like me were basically anti-tragic, we were captivated by the Bannon books, astounded to discover there had been bars and friends and girlfriends and mirrors even in the pre-liberation days—and maybe it was the Ann Bannon piece that inspired Andrea to begin her own lesbian soap opera, Random Lust. In the first sentence, the main character, Jo Burke, "paused at the entrance of the Select Bar, ran her work-worn yet well-shaped hand through her short, neat auburn hair, and casually shrugged her aged black leather jacket in place." Andrea and I, as her editor, found these adjectival descriptions of Jo endlessly amusing; they appear in every episode: "No one could guess the fierce tumult that raged beneath that tough, almost hard, high-cheek-boned face with its lines of experience, sorrow and wisdom, beneath that almost arrogant thrust of her lean hips." "Women . . . ah, women," Jo meditates. "A crisp meter maid in her little blue uniform neatly ticketed cars with a sexy flick of her pen . . . A silky-haired Harvard co-ed, clutching an expensive, extinct-lizard briefcase . . . And an elegant older woman, whose fur coat brushed against Jo's waiting lips." Random Lust became wildly popular with our readers, except of course with those who found it silly and objectifying.

Andrea invited me to visit her apartment, where colorful antique quilts leaking batting decorated the walls. In her kitchen hung a yellowing flyer in her loopy handwriting advertising a reading from her first novel. I wished I could have sat among the circle of rapt listeners depicted in the drawing on the flyer, but the event was long over, the novel discarded. It all existed only in her enviable past. She was at work on another novel now, the characters based on the women she had met while teaching at the women's prison in Framingham. It was being rejected by publishers everywhere, who found the prison setting alienating. "Couldn't you change it to a school? Wait, how about this: A hospital!" I begged to read it; she gave me stacks of manuscript to take home. It was brilliant.

Then Andrea did something even more wonderful than live in her disheveled apartment in Cambridgeport—she rented a house on an island in Maine's Casco Bay for the summer, and she invited me to visit. I first traveled to Cliff Island with Michael Bronski and Walta Borawski. Since they usually preferred not to leave Boston, the trip was an adventure they would have undertaken only for Andrea, with whom they had both fallen instantly in love, almost as I had. Walta snapped a roll of photographs to prove we had visited her little white house, sat in her garden, and sunned ourselves on the rocks at the beach where she swam.

I visited Andrea a second time, without the guys. I took a bus from Boston to Portland, and a ferry that made a circuit of all the islands. Betsy and I had been together for a little less than a year. Andrea and I were taking an evening stroll on the island when we saw lights and commotion. She rushed us down to the town landing, to the same place where my ferry had docked. A man had been taken ill, and the fireboat roared up to transport him to the hospital in Portland. We watched for a long time as the man was wheeled out on a stretcher and loaded onto the bobbing boat. Would he survive? We never found out. Andrea wrote a poem about the incident, dedicated to me. It's about how the emergency in the foggy night was like a dream, and the collision between Andrea and me dreamlike too, according to her—silent, befogged, and inevitable. No one had ever dedicated a poem to me before, not even Betsy, although she had instantly responded to my valentine with a sweet homemade one of her own. I must have enough love in my heart for two, I thought.

Predictably, once Andrea and I were back on the mainland, she took up with someone else almost immediately, and I was relegated to weekday evenings and occasional Sunday afternoons. This went on for months. Once, we went cross-country skiing together in Lincoln, where she had grown up, and although I'm not very skilled and tend to fall down a lot, she praised my stamina. The snow was powdery and the suburban woods quiet and beautiful. Back in Cambridge we got into bed and pulled Andrea's colorful comforter over us, and in the morning she left early and I showered alone, using her shampoo, although I suspected it of causing my rash. I was so obsessed, so overcome by Andrea that I couldn't help talking about her to everyone—Michael and Walta, my mother. I had the crazy idea that she would praise me because Andrea was Jewish. "*German Jewish,* Ma." For my mother, the phenomenon of the old immigrant rivalries surfacing among lesbians must have been too bizarre to contemplate.

I learned to make Greek salad the way Andrea did, heavy on the salty ingredients like feta and olives and marinated artichoke hearts, light on the lettuce. She couldn't abide bananas, the scent of them ripening in a basket on top of the refrigerator, as they did in my kitchen. I wrote her a poem about her food preferences:

> "Your nipples are like cherries," I tell you.
> "I don't like fruit," you say.

I had traveled to her island and run willingly off the cliff, although I knew I would not remain suspended in air for long. Andrea had been dropping me every second we were together, and one day, she finally dropped me altogether. And then Betsy broke up with me too. The whole situation had gotten out of hand, and I discovered a big disadvantage of smashing monogamy, which is that multiple simultaneous relationships can result in multiple simultaneous breakups. Really I've always been more suited to one person at a time. After a long and tearful conversation, Betsy and I hugged goodbye, and as I walked down her front steps she called to me from the doorway, "Amy, we'll be flirting with each other until we're eighty." So far, she's been right.

Richard introduced me to Urvashi Vaid. He had met her on his first day of law school, in the student lounge, where she had been ostentatiously reading a copy of *GCN*, hoping to flush out the other gay students. I hadn't even figured out her name—Irv? like an old Jewish guy?—when Betsy's socialist-feminist study group decided to hold a conference about the state of women's liberation, a term that was starting to sound quaint even in 1981. I didn't want *not* to go just because Betsy was peripherally involved, and every time I wandered into a workshop, there was Urvashi, catching my eye and patting the empty chair next to her.

The next week she invited me to her house for dinner. When I arrived she had a million pots going on the stove and was flying around the kitchen making Indian bread, flattening little balls of dough between her palms and frying them in a special little round-bottomed, cast-iron pan. At just the right moment, she pressed them gently around the edges with the tips of her fingers, and—poof!—the *chappatis* puffed up full of air.

"Wow," I said.

"I do it all the time," Urv promised seductively.

I've known Urvashi for decades by now, during which I've watched her cook innumerable delicious Indian dinners—but never *chappatis*. Never again has she gotten out the little cast-iron pan, at least not for me.

At the women's liberation conference, the room had been hung with a banner: "An Army of Lovers Cannot Fail." A woman sitting next to me and Urvashi leaned over and whispered, "What about an army of ex-lovers?" It was the first time we'd heard that joke, and we thought it was hysterical.

11

The Nude Boy Controversy

In 1980, after I'd been features editor for two years, Richard left *GCN* to go to law school, and I was promoted to his position of managing editor—that is, if it's possible to receive a promotion when everyone is, theoretically, co-equal.

I inherited the managing editor's desk—a grand, oak partner affair with kneeholes and drawers on both sides, designed, I suppose, for exceptionally compatible partners, who didn't mind staring at each other all day. Richard had used every inch of the vast desktop himself. With his long arm coiling around the paper, he would left-handedly cover one legal pad after another with his big angular print, occasionally reaching to peck something out on the typewriter he had placed at arm's length beyond his writing area. Beyond the typewriter he'd arranged stacks of paper, envelopes, newspaper clippings, and pink while-you-were-out slips in configurations inscrutable to anyone else, although he claimed to know precisely the contents and priority of every scrap in every pile.

Before he left, he asked me to help him pack. He insisted that rather than sweep his papers off the desk and into a trash can, I transfer them carefully into boxes. These he dragged back to his apartment and stored in the kitchen cabinets, empty as they were of cooking supplies. When he left Boston for New York City in 1986, he restashed the papers in a four-drawer filing cabinet, which after some protest I agreed to keep in my basement. At first when he visited he would go downstairs and come back up with a few old magazines or a folder of letters. But he hadn't touched his

GayCommunityNews

Vol. 8, No. 17   (617) 426-4469   ©GCN, 1980   November 15, 1980

Where Do We Go From Here?
'A Disaster For The Movement'

By Jil Clark

"A disaster to lesbian and gay rights and the women's movement." That's how Lucia Valeska of the National Gay Task Force (NGTF) described the grim outcome of the national election. In the aftermath, GCN interviewed numerous lesbian, gay and feminist political organizers. Most were not surprised by right-wing Republican Ronald Reagan's victory and all but the Reagan supporters were disturbed by the large margin by which his machine vaulted him into the Oval Office. The landslide conservative Republican victory in the Senate, on the other hand, shocked conservative and liberal alike.

Foremost on the minds of progressive lesbians and gays is the blow that will probably be dealt to us in the U.S. Supreme Court, where as many as four judges may be stepping down during Reagan's term — unless they move to resign immediately so that lame-duck President Jimmy Carter can make

the appointments. Viewed from this angle, the cause of human rights may incur more severe damage from Reagan's election than from the conservative coup in the Senate; a Supreme Court appointment is good for the life of the judge, whereas a Senate seat is up for grabs every six years.

"As far as Reagan's promise to appoint a woman to the Supreme Court . . . well, Phyllis Schlafly is a lawyer," commented Ann Maguire of the Massachusetts Gay Political Caucus.

Many lesbians and gay men fear that the movement's loss of accessibility to the White House will result in the loss of some hard-won influence in Congress and loss of the dialogue which had been initiated with the Immigration and Naturalization Service. Within hours of Carter's concession speech, a defeated-sounding Valeska commented only that "the White House project has been going on for several years. We (NGTF) will try to maintain it.

The outlook is not good."

Steve Endean of the Gay Rights National Lobby (GRNL) assured GCN the fate of the lesbian and gay rights bills now in the Senate and in a House committee is unaffected by the election, since they are not expected to be made into law for years, in any case. All but two of the sponsors of the bills who were up for reelection were returned to Washington — several, such as Jim Weaver of Oregon, having survived vigorous challenges by born-agains.

However, Endean and other lobbyists will have their defense work cut out for them for the next four years or more. "We'll see more anti-gay, McDonald-type amendments in Congress. Unless we can mobilize more effectively, their chances of passing will increase, not decrease," he said. Understandably, many lesbian and gay progressive leaders assume the conservative victories reflect a general trend toward the

Continued on page 7

filing cabinet for years when, in 2000, Roberta and I decided to move and cleaned the basement. I put Richard's filing cabinet—his meeting minutes on legal paper now faded from yellow to beige, his telephone messages unanswered since 1979—out with the rest of the trash. When I told him what I'd done, he regretted vigorously that he had stored his gay historical documents with a custodian who'd shown them so little respect.

As managing editor, Richard had a happy confidence in his own authority, whereas I suffered from the feminine desperation to be universally beloved. I hated myself for it. My reluctance to force an issue, which I tried to rationalize to myself as compassionate and democratic, undoubtedly contributed to the paper's slide from being a *collective*, where the rule is dedication, trust, and respect for one and all, to what I call a *corrupted collective*. In the collective, no one has power over anyone else, and the members make all decisions together—in a kind of sack race, where you're tied to another contestant and must devise a means of joint locomotion. It's inherently silly-looking and inefficient and places you far too close to your partner, so her sweat soaks you and her breath puffs into your face as you hop together toward the goal. In contrast, in the corrupted collective, no one has power over anyone else, and the members bound off however and wherever they want. You don't tell anyone what you're planning until it's too late to stop you.

The early 1980s were depressing years at the paper, like one long November. Ronald Reagan in the White House. AIDS on its way. Rain, wind, and low gray clouds. *GCN* had always frustrated and offended its readers, not to mention the staff and volunteers, and enraged subscribers wrote to us weekly to rant about how we were destroying the movement: We were sexist. We were racist. We were pedophiles. We were Communists. We were pornographers. We were closet queens. We were tasteless. We were irrational. We couldn't spell. We pandered to the Democratic Party. Our jokes weren't funny. We said *dykes and faggots* instead of *lesbians and gay men*. We quoted your ex who is a miserable excuse for a human being.

The letters columns of the early eighties were more crowded than ever with harangues about obscure points of disagreement among members of minuscule if not completely nonexistent socialist parties or, confusingly, similar debates among fans of rival lesbian folk musicians. Our coverage swung haphazardly from the outrageous to the doctrinaire, sometimes managing to be both at once, as with the grotesque cover that featured a hyper-realistic drawing of a penis wrapped in barbed wire. It horrified absolutely everyone who opened the paper, except the art director and his cadre. They said they were delighted to have published such a meticulous and technically accomplished artwork and implied that the objections came from people who were just too squeamish for gay liberation.

The nude boy controversy was one I'd forgotten completely until I started reading through the old newspapers. I turned a stiff, yellowing page, and there was Michael Thompson, beautiful, smiling, long-haired, striding naked out of the ocean after a refreshing morning swim, the water lapping at his thighs—and suddenly the old feeling swamped me, the wrench in the gut of panic and shame. Michael was more often photographer than subject, and on the page along with the photo of him were pictures he had taken of other beautiful boys, younger than he, one stretched out on the sand in all his glory, another blonde, sleepy-eyed, and so pretty that a wild seabird had actually flown down and perched on his finger.

The photos were originally meant to illustrate Michael's article on nude beaches, which he'd been assigned to write for the Provincetown supplement. Although the supplement's purpose was to encourage advertising—not to mention to provide the advertising manager with a free trip to Provincetown—the gay guesthouse owners and shopkeepers had little interest in publicizing or even acknowledging the existence of Provincetown's nude beach. In their view it was a simply a source of bad vacation experiences for their customers, who in their quest for an all-over tan might easily find themselves confronted with an overheated park ranger in full regalia, from shiny black boots to safari hat, writing out a fifty-dollar ticket. A persistent rumor had it that the rangers were Mormons especially recruited for the job. The Mormons dreamed of converting the gay men, and the gay men dreamed of converting the Mormons, back in the underbrush of the National Seashore dunes—and who, I wonder, was more successful?

When the Thursday night layout volunteers were given Michael's photos to crop and size for the printer there was a terrible blow-up. Several lesbians, ignoring the strategically placed ocean waves and accidents of posture and focus, objected to reproducing photos of naked men flashing their penises, which they said were liable to offend and even terrify women. The penis, they maintained, represents nothing less than the unadorned source of patriarchal power, and coming across it unexpectedly might cause some lesbians to re-experience traumatic abuse perpetrated by people with similar organs. The gay men felt differently about the penis, of course, but they mostly refrained from emphasizing their views, reluctant to cause further offense. Our promotions manager, Maida Tilchen, who spent much of her time writing articles that determined, through the use of textual, fashion, and ticket-price analysis, whether various lesbian musicians had sold out, precipitating all those letters from their fans, was particularly outraged. "Lesbians don't want to look at *that*," she said. But why? others responded. Were we ashamed of our bodies? Were not photos of nude boys perfectly appropriate in an article about nude beaches?

As the argument wore on I brooded over my lack of sensitivity. Unlike the debaters surrounding me, I *had* seen the photos in advance. They'd given me a moment's pause, but then I'd gotten distracted by something or other. Bomb threats coming in over the telephone. Staff members threatening to quit. Letters to be written to subscribers begging for donations to pay our health insurance premiums. Once again I had betrayed my sisters. It was midnight, the paper had to be sent off to the printer any minute, and everyone was yelling at one another and crying.

—Oh no, a letter from *GCN*, and I bet they want *money* again!

—None of the other papers I read hit me up for contributions twice a year. Times are hard for me, too! Why can't *GCN* make it on ads and subscriptions?

—Did you ever try to sell an ad for a lesbian and gay publication? It's not easy. A lot of straight businesses don't want to be associated with a gay paper. Even some gay business owners are afraid an ad in *GCN* will mean coming out. Or they think *GCN*'s too controversial. Although you probably *like* that.

—Well, sure I do. My dear, those letters! I like the way they cover lesbian *and* gay men's issues. So do lots of people. Why can't they survive on subs? They charge 25 bucks a year for them. That's about all I can afford.

—Did you know the PO raised their mailing rates by *a third* in January with *no warning*? Printing costs have climbed 20% in the last year and a half. And they have to pay the rent, and salaries, and insurance, and the brown envelope bill, and the typesetter, and of course refreshments for the volunteers. They just about break even on subs.

—What about newsstands? I once saw *GCN* in a bookstore in Lawrence, Kansas. They get around.

—It's a good way to get the word out, but as far as money goes, it's peanuts!

Face it. It would be a bleak world without *GCN* to look forward to every week. We're trying our best to keep costs down, revenues up, and subscription prices affordable. We're beginning to raise money now for a down-payment on the purchase of our own typesetting equipment. Owning our own equipment will enable us to keep our typesetting costs low, make our layout process more efficient, and make *GCN* more beautiful. To keep a bigger, better and more financially stable *GCN* coming out every week, we need your support.

Sincerely,
Bob Andrews, Richard Burns, Kevin Cathcart,
Beth Kelly, Cindy Rizzo, Eric Rofes,
Urvashi Vaid, Nancy Wechsler
The *GCN* Board of Directors

Gay Community News

Please send us your check or money order, or fill out the VISA/Mastercharge form below. A return envelope is enclosed.

I am donating
- ☐ $5
- ☐ $10
- ☐ $25
- ☐ $50
- ☐ $100
- ☐ $250

**22 BROMFIELD ST,
BOSTON, MASS.,02108
617-426-4469**

Name_____
Account No._____
Expiration Date_____
Signature_____
☐ VISA   ☐ Mastercharge

Why, as managing editor, didn't I simply step in and say, "Do this," "Do that"—"Run the nude boys!" "Kill the barbed-wire penis!" Maybe because, when you're at the center of the universe, the importance of every little thing is magnified tenfold and freighted with overweening consequence. The exaggerated gravitational pull prevents you from finding a purchase anywhere, a solid place where you could raise a thing before you and turn it about to contemplate its substance and structure.

Ironically, I'd previously been accused of being a moralist. During a dispute over whether or not the opening of a new gay bar was newsworthy, Charles Ash declared that Richard and I, who argued that it was not, were nothing but a pair of Methodist ministers, who objected automatically any time a person wanted to have a little fun. Charles, one of *GCN*'s older volunteers, came in once a week to work on our articles index, his handwriting shaky in blue ink on the white cards. The articles listed in Charles's index were never the ones we were looking for, they were completely unfamiliar, in fact, but Charles was dedicated to his project. His image of Richard and me as ministers was so incongruous that no one could come up with anything to say in our defense, and Michael Thompson was dispatched to take a photo of the bar's grand opening. On one wall of the dance floor there was a fancy neon sign that flashed alternately the name of the bar, BUDDIES, and the word GAY, and when Mayor Kevin White, a crony of the manager, showed up to welcome people to his friend's new establishment, Michael used up a whole roll of film frantically and ultimately successfully trying to freeze-frame the mayor in front of the sign flashing GAY.

Eventually we worked out a compromise over the nude boy photos—a typical *GCN* compromise, in that it was bound to offend people on all sides of the issue. It might even have been my idea; it was the kind of thing I would have come up with. We yanked the pictures from the resort supplement, distorting and confusing the design so that in the end hardly anyone actually made it all the way through Michael's article. Then—this is the genius part—we *published* the photos the following week, with commentaries pro and con by Michael, staff members, and layout volunteers. A final note invited readers to weigh in, not that they needed an engraved invitation.

What struck me when I came upon the photos again after all these years was what we'd left out of our debates. The anti-photo contingent objected to the images on the grounds that they were looksist, able-bodyist, ageist, racist, and sexist, and that despite Michael's claim that he had simply recorded what he saw, a photographer strolling along a nude beach would encounter not a clique of young, humpy, white guys posing on the sand but rather a motley crowd of people of various generations, ethnicities, and degrees of obesity. In publishing such misleading photos, the argument continued, *GCN* was guilty of perpetuating the destructive values of advertising and the mainstream media, which had caused so many of us to feel inadequate about our bodies and our sexuality. Our news editor, David Morris, wrote that he liked the photos, yet in the end he had decided he opposed publishing them, reflecting in his laid-back, ex-hippie way,

> I have been naked among other naked people, friends and strangers, in several different settings and have found a kind of personal liberation in it. . . . I have lost my self-consciousness and shame to the degree that the setting included a variety of human beings, all with the same kind of self-consciousness to lose and all losing it because in the diversity one's own naked body has turned out to be as unremarkable as any, as flawed as the rest in its own way and as beautiful.

The pro-photo commentators, on the other hand, extolled the pictures' aesthetic and technical virtues and the pleasure they gave to the viewer. Rather than make viewers feel insecure about their bodies, they said, the photos celebrated the natural charm of the gay male form.

But no one came right out with the obvious. *The photos were sexy.* Of course they made everybody itchy. The principled discussion of looksism, aesthetics, the state of nature, and even racism and sexism was really beside the point. I didn't mind a little erotica, or even porn, defined as we did at *GCN*, as material created for the specific, utilitarian purpose of sexual arousal. Porn was, after all, but one fairly minor manifestation of the infinite creativity of human beings in the area of sexual expression, which is so lavish that one might argue that all creativity springs from this source, this experience of agency and joy. In fact, at one time, I myself published a sort of porno magazine, *Bad Attitude*, with my then girlfriend. It was for lesbians, so it was a little text-heavy; in fact, it included not only porno stories but also, in keeping with my girlfriend's proclivities, dense theoretical analyses of why such stories, written by and for lesbians, were unique and significant. The problem was, they weren't really. Secretly, I found them embarrassing. It was amazing how many people wanted to be pushed around by teachers, camp counselors, or basketball coaches—and then there are so many cute names for the genitals. I had thought that went out with Lady Chatterley. Eventually my girlfriend and I got bored with *Bad Attitude* and turned it over to a collective of feminist sadomasochists—which is either a contradiction in terms or the only kind of collective there is.

But *GCN* stood out from most gay publications exactly because we didn't publish sexy pictures to attract readers, and we didn't make most

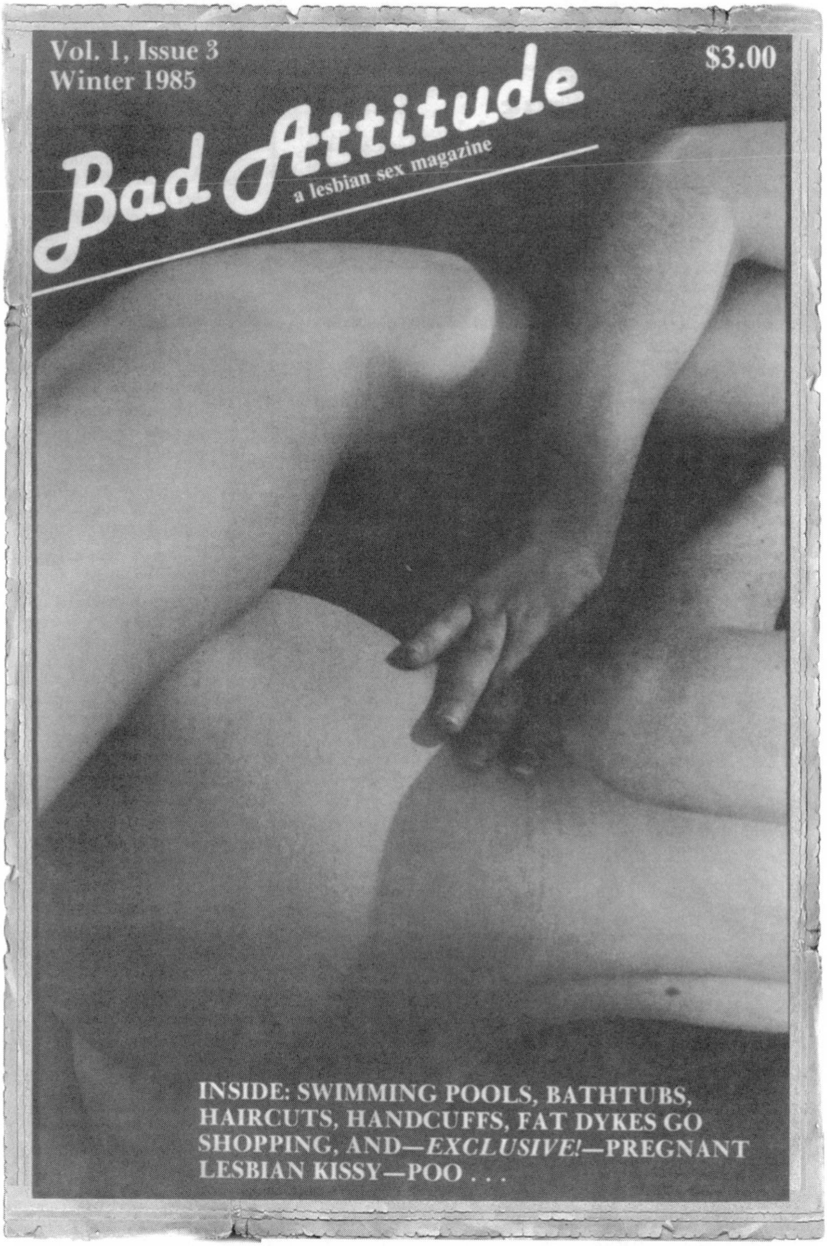

Vol. 1, Issue 3
Winter 1985

$3.00

Bad Attitude

a lesbian sex magazine

INSIDE: SWIMMING POOLS, BATHTUBS, HAIRCUTS, HANDCUFFS, FAT DYKES GO SHOPPING, AND—*EXCLUSIVE!*—PREGNANT LESBIAN KISSY—POO . . .

of our income from gay bar ads and personal classifieds—which may be part of the reason we were able to retain our mixed-gender readership and staff, since lesbians and gay men obviously have different interests in these areas. In contrast, it was well known that the *Advocate*, as much as the publishers might tout its respectability, professionalism, audited circulation figures, and quest for national advertisers, actually made its profits from its Pink Pages, the insert that carried the personals.

Whereas *GCN* had Mousie. Every week Nancy Walker, our classified ad manager, published a piece of doggerel addressed to her beloved "Mousie Mousie Wildflower." After Mousie finished graduate school the headline changed for a while to "Mousie Mousie Ph.D." The week *GCN* published the nude boy photos, the Mousie, a classic, read:

> MOUSIE MOUSIE WILDFLOWER
> We finally went to the fair
> But the fair was only fair
> But not as fair as thou art fair
> Oh wonderful wondrous fair.
> I love you more than coconuts!
> All my love, Porcupine.

To the continual bewilderment of the rest of the staff, our readers admired Porcupine's verse. They even imitated it, creating a nursery ambience that probably thwarted the possibility of our ever making a killing selling sex ads.

And as far as bar ads, the other solid source of revenue for most gay papers, *GCN* had been founded in part as a protest *against* gay bars, whose straight, possibly Mafia owners profited from our oppression. Gay bars were dark, expensive, and unhealthy. They encouraged alcoholism, shame, and the life of the closet. They were secret, romantic, and fun. You never knew what would happen or who you would meet. We criticized them, but at night we patronized them every chance we got.

We were pro-sex but anti-exploitation, and it should be easy to tell the difference, but it isn't. We didn't want to do anything that would seem to be suppressing sexuality, like refusing to publish pictures of nude boys; but we didn't want to do anything that would perpetuate the old, oppressive values, like publishing pictures of nude boys. So, to circumvent our confusion, we talked about *looksism* instead of sexiness—and *ageism* instead of the boys' age.

In Maida's commentary condemning the photos, she said, "I could give a long theoretical analysis of why this group of photos does not belong in a feminist newspaper, but I trust that *GCN* readers either know this stuff already or perhaps will be motivated by this discussion to research it for themselves." I ran into Maida recently. Unlike me, she has always remembered the nude boy controversy, and she's given it quite a bit of thought. She told me her first reaction to the photos in fact had nothing to do with her research on sexism, racism, etc. It was: "I'm not going to jail for *that!*" She didn't bring this up, she said, because she was afraid of getting yelled at (which was worse, apparently, than taking the rap as a promoter of kiddie porn).

I'd prefer to gloss over this issue of the boys' age, the photographer's slightly greater age, the ethical questions of exploitation and consent, and various legalities, but unfortunately, in his own commentary on the photos, Michael was completely frank about the circumstances in which he took them. The boy with the bird, he wrote, was "a runaway doing quaaludes supplied by a gay man." Michael! Did you never hear of *too much information*? But of course not. TMI is a phrase of the 1990s, of the Internet, of Monica Lewinsky and her thong. In the 1970s we were coming out of the closet and opening all doors, including the doors of perception. We were telling all. Amazingly, no one on the staff, and none of the letter writers, bothered to comment on the situation Michael described. Yet we couldn't have supported plying young people with drugs—could we?

But *we* were young people. Few of us had been out of high school long enough not to feel relieved at each birthday that marked the passing of time between that hideous experience and our present situation. There was virtually no age difference between most of us at *GCN* and Maya and Shannon, for example, two runaways who lived up on Fort Hill and helped out with *FagRag*, or George Smith, the president of Boston Area Gay and Lesbian Youth. It just depended on how you wanted to define yourself. We were publishing a national newspaper, which put us more on the grown-up side of things. Still, the boys in Michael's photographs were probably not so much objects to many of us as subjects. Stretching out in the sun on the beach, looking good, feeling good, sex in the offing—it didn't look like exploitation, it didn't look like a bad time at all.

Growing up, everything we ever heard about gay sexuality was lies, lies, lies.

That is, if we had heard anything at all. Words were hard to come by. You started exploring the love that dare not speak its name by furtively looking up "homosexual" in the dictionary. When I was in junior high school, one of my teachers bizarrely advised me to read the letters of Tchaikovsky, who was in constant agony over a mysterious problem he called "It"—a term I couldn't even look up.

So as gay liberationists we had to start by questioning absolutely everything, from day one and that inevitable inquiry about the baby in the stroller: "Is it a boy or a girl?" Just try to stop yourself from asking—you can't, you have to find out. But why do you need to know? Why were some people in and some out, some up, some down? Pink, blue, black, white—who made all these rules, and whom did they serve? Why were some forms of human touch sanctioned, even venerated, and others forbidden and accursed? We had to start all over again figuring out what was right and what was wrong, because our ethical assumptions had been handed down to us by people who were liars, oppressors, and thieves.

I wrote a Speaking Out op-ed essay after I'd been at *GCN* for three months, about the crash course I'd just received in lesbian and gay politics and sexuality. My brief time at the paper, I said, had "shaken me up emotionally, intellectually, morally and politically." I rambled on for a while about the value of not looking for answers: "Listening yields no answers, only some questions," I said. "Process may be hard to live with, but most of the time, it's all we've got." Before I'd heard my new friends' coming-out stories, both those who described the cruelties they'd experienced at the hands of other teenage boys and those who claimed that their adult encounters with young men were mentoring relationships of the kind so admired by the ancient Greeks, I had thought the issue of intergenerational sex was a no-brainer: let the kids have sex with other kids. Grownups, get out of the way. But finally I ventured what was for me the big insight: "It may, paradoxically, feel safer to a boy to experiment sexually with men who are strangers than with his peers, who could turn against him as soon as anyone whispers the accusation 'faggot.'"

When I wrote my essay in early 1979, the gay community was still reeling from the Revere Sex-Ring panic the previous year, when Suffolk County District Attorney Garrett Byrne, who was running for re-election, had charged twenty-four men in the working class city of Revere with operating a massive boy-prostitution business. Some of the men admitted they'd had what they said were consensual relationships with teenagers, and some insisted they'd done nothing at all. Byrne set up a "hotline" requesting tips about gay men—anonymity guaranteed, just tell us who they are. The Boston/Boise Committee (named, to remind us that these things followed a pattern, after an infamous 1950s sex-ring scare in Boise, Idaho) formed to attempt to counteract the hysteria about the cases in the media, especially in the *Boston Herald American*, and to ensure fair trials for the Revere defendants—no small task when venturing any sort of opinion meant instant guilt by association. (Realizing that the Revere cases were only particularly sensational examples of gay people's inability to get a fair hearing in the courts, in 1978 members of Boston/Boise went on to found GLAD, Gay and Lesbian Advocates and Defenders, with Richard as its first president and John Ward as executive director.) The cases caused a massive split in the gay community, and the sides often seemed to line up by gender: gay men supporting Boston/Boise and lesbians taking the charges against the Revere defendants at face value and even refusing to see anything problematic about the tip line soliciting anonymous denunciations of gay men (Elaine Noble actually endorsed it).

Lesbians declared that "lesbians don't do that," echoing the old Gertrude Steinish prejudice, at least as reported by Hemingway, to whom Gertrude opined,

> The act male homosexuals commit is ugly and repugnant and afterwards they are disgusted with themselves. They drink and take drugs, to palliate this, but they are disgusted with the act and they are always changing partners and cannot be really happy. . . . In women it is the opposite. They do nothing that they are disgusted by and nothing that is repulsive and afterwards they are happy and they can lead happy lives together.

Men do an "act," while women do "nothing . . . nothing." There's a strain of lesbian culture that thinks of lesbian sex as pure, spiritual nearly to the point of nonexistence. The homophobic corollary to Freud's famous, sexist question, "What do women want?"—answer: everything—is "What do lesbians do?"—answer: nothing. In the seventies, encouraged by this notion of lesbian sex and nothingness, some women declared themselves "political lesbians" or "woman-identified women" (or, to get the "man" out of it completely, "womyn-identified," "womb-moon-identified," etc.). "Any woman can." You didn't even have to muss your hair, although you might want to put on a plaid flannel shirt. These political lesbians had a tendency suddenly to drop out of sight and turn up a few weeks later, married. "As I understand it," concluded writer Pat (now Patrick, but that's another story) Califia in frustration, "after the wimmin's revolution, sex will consist of wimmin holding hands, taking their shirts off and dancing in a circle. Then we will all fall asleep at exactly the same moment."

Of course in real life, lesbians, like everyone else, were happily having all kinds of sex all over the place. *GCN* published an account, submitted in response to my essay, of the writer's relationship, as a teenager, with her aunt, which she still looked back upon with great affection and even nostalgia. Even among my own small circle I knew of at least one women who had had a torrid, incredibly romantic affair with her high school English teacher, with whom she'd traveled to Europe. Others had lovers who were ten or fifteen years older than they were. At what point does sex become "intergenerational," anyway?

Socialists said that those with nothing to lose shall rise up, and feminists added that it was all about who wielded the power. As I searched for new politics and ethics, my allies were the entire alphabet of those whom society had cast out: abused women, black people, cross-dressers, disabled people, environmentalists, feminists, gays, homeless people, hermaphrodites, immigrants, Jews, kinsey sixes, lunatics, marxists, nerds, nattering nabobs of negativism, organizers, pacifists, pederasts, pedestrians, poor people, pornographers, prisoners, prostitutes, queens, Rastafarians, sadomasochists, trannies, Unitarians, vegetarians, welfare mothers, ex-lovers, youth, zoophiles.

So when the police raided Michael Thompson's house and arrested him for having more photographs of nude boys than seemed humanly possible, I contributed $300 to his bail fund. Then, on the very morning when I had combed my hair and put on a blazer and readied myself to go to court to testify, as someone who had hired Michael, to his good character and professionalism, his case was suddenly dismissed. Something was clearly fishy about the whole incident—both the raid and the dismissal—and I never figured out what, but no matter. I had no doubt that Michael was the gentle, honest person I'd been prepared to swear him to be. I could not conceive that any friend or even acquaintance of mine could turn out to be anything but.

For all my advocacy of process, questioning, the complexity of truth, and the necessity of tolerating contradictions, once I had made my alliances, I held off looking much further: arrests of gay men were homophobic witch-hunts; and lesbians who warned about exploitation had an important point of course but basically were covering up for their fearful, antisex attitudes.

Many years later, I was working on a committee that was organizing the Out/Write gay writers' conference in Boston. A fellow committee member made what was to me a familiar, stomach-knotting request— that we include in the conference program a statement of support for NAMBLA (North American Man-Boy Love Association) members, whom he said were being unfairly hounded by the media and even arrested for their sexual proclivities. To try to prove to us the harmlessness of their desires, he passed around a NAMBLA newsletter. Boys of color from who knows what developing countries, photographed who knows where, under who knows what horrific circumstances. Also, for some reason, Scandinavians in bathing suits. I glanced through the pages and flipped the newsletter quickly to the next person in the circle—the way children swat away the ball in their game of hot potato—as if holding it would implicate me. But I couldn't prevent myself from seeing the pictures clearly enough this time to realize how naïve I'd once been, to assume everyone in my alphabet was so good.

12

God Bless the Child

Mel Horne said he'd been kicked out of every gay bar in town, so he'd have to decline the kind invitation to go to Sporters with the Thursday night layout volunteers. It was just as well, he said, the bars were exploiters, taking our money, encouraging addiction and looksism. He'd go home to Doug, his boyfriend, crawl into bed with a good book, and go out like a light.

I assumed I'd misheard the part about his getting kicked out of bars, or that it was yet another gay male joke flying over my head, since Mel had laughed when he said it, although without much hope that anyone else would find it funny—he always seemed to have an undertow of sadness tugging at him. I couldn't imagine him doing anything that would get him kicked out of anywhere, much less a gay bar.

Mel's desk was next to mine when I first started working at the paper, and he and I talked and talked all day long about everything under the sun—our families, the hidden injuries of class and the foibles of gay men (favorites of Mel's), literature, politics, sociology (Mel had some credits toward a graduate degree), and the homely art of crochet. My mother had taught it to me, and she'd also taught it to my brother, hoping to keep us occupied on rainy summer afternoons, but I'd never known a grown man to do it. Periodically, Richard would glare at me from his desk across the room, implying that I should leave Mel alone. Mel was *GCN*'s promotions manager, and Richard felt about him the same way he felt about every promotions manager the paper ever had; he was convinced that we would have thousands more subscribers if only, just once, we'd hire a promo-homo who would do a little work.

Mel was thirty-six when we met in 1978, ten years older than I, and our age difference felt huge. Even though we were working together on a gay newspaper, I don't think gay liberation seemed quite real to Mel; so much of his gay experience had taken place before it came along. He clearly remembered the week of Stonewall in late June 1969, he told me. He'd heard the shocking dish on the dance floor at Fire Island Pines—not about the riots, no one was talking about those, but about the death of Judy Garland. He had been a beautiful, barefoot, overall-wearing hippie, with long auburn hair and a rich older boyfriend.

Like a wayward son, the gay movement, with its lapses into classism, racism, sexism, was forever disappointing Mel. He proudly called himself a feminist—despite some controversy in the office and, in fact, all over town about whether men could be feminists or whether they should be satisfied with being *pro-feminists.* After the first Women-Take-Back-the-Night demonstration for women's safety, some of the marchers had gotten together to write an angry letter to the women's newspaper *Sojourner*— not to *GCN,* of course, because it was so male, but the letter concerned some of the *GCN* men. The writers were sick and tired of contingents of so-called "male feminists" standing on the sidelines holding candles, thus exciting the marchers' applause—men as usual demanding women's attention and sapping their energy. In the next issue someone wrote back and quashed the argument, saying that as a woman strong in mind and body she could handle a little clapping with no dizziness, palpitations, or noticeable diminution of energy whatsoever.

Mel didn't consider himself to be all man, anyway. He preferred the term *sissy,* as in his headline for an article he wrote on a new trend in psychotherapy: "Once I Was a Sissy, Now I'm a Gender-Discord Boy." As a child he had played dress-up in his mother's closet.

This is how I remember the coming-out story he told me:

In New Haven, where Mel went to high school, there was a park where the football players used to go when they wanted to beat up a queer. Mel had known he was a queer since the day his crazy mother had curled his hair into gorgeous red ringlets in honor of his first Holy Communion and in church he had gazed into the young priest's gray eyes as the priest placed the host carefully right in the middle of his tongue. So Mel decided, if the park is where the queers go, I shall go there. He sat down on a bench and waited, and after a while a balding

BIPAD: 65498

ISSN: 0147-0728

gay community news

VOL. 6, NO. 6   AUG. 26/SEPT. 2, 1978   THE GAY WEEKLY 50¢

wo
un

take back
the night

Cover illustration by Sheryl M. Williams

GCN'S BOOK REVIEW
STUDENTS LOSE IN OKLAHOMA
WHY LESBIANS FIGHT VIOLENCE

man, pudgy around the middle, wearing tan chinos that were a little too short and pulled awkwardly around his crotch, sat down next to Mel and offered him a cigarette.

"I've never seen you here before," he said. "Do you go to college?"

"Yes, college," said Mel, a little sorry about the lie.

The man looked him up and down and then stood up, and Mel thought he was going to leave, but he took Mel's hand and pulled him from the bench, and before he led him back into the dark bushes he kissed him on the cheek.

"Don't worry, darling," he said. "We'll go very, very slowly."

Mel said that on this issue, at least, the FagRaggers had a point: he had experienced only kindness from the older men he encountered in the park, and only abuse from his peers and family.

In the summer of 1979, before the lesbian and gay march on Washington, Mel had suddenly become enthusiastic about making a *GCN* banner. He proposed a design in three sections, our logo in black lettering on white muslin, just as it appeared every week on the masthead, but bordered in pink, so that when assembled, the banner would form the shape of a pink triangle—if you happened to be looking down on it from above. He rushed out to Chinatown and bought the fabric, which then gathered dust on his desk for months. Finally, the week before the march, Raymond Hopkins, who was the sort of reliable person who could be counted on to show up every Friday to stuff envelopes and to bring a main dish to potlucks, took it home and sewed two sections of it in accordance with Mel's design. The third section, which was to have defined the triangle, was never completed.

I once wrote a short story about Mel, in which he drinks beer in the office all afternoon, as he sometimes did, since we often kept beer in the refrigerator for the Thursday night layout volunteers, the only rule being to keep it and all snacks off the light tables to prevent them from spilling onto the boards. Then he unfurls the leftover bolts of fabric on his desk and transforms them into drag, wrapping himself in a gown of white muslin with an elegant black shawl. He constructs a high pink turban, which he fastens with a paperclip.

"Love the hat!" I shriek.

"What do you know about it." Sneering, Mel brushes me aside and with a hand on his hip strides down the stairs. Out in the street the throngs of shoppers heading for Filene's part before him like the Red Sea.

Mel Horne.
Photo by Michael Thompson

The episode of the turban never happened, no matter how clearly I can see that paperclip above his ear and the view out the front window of the people making way before him—as they will, sometimes, for madness or other spectacle. Mel left our office quite differently.

We were having a big membership meeting. The membership was a vestigial structure left over from the early days when *GCN* was published by a true collective of volunteers, before we had paid staffers with job titles and even a board of directors with a president and an executive committee. The membership, whose role was to make decisions about broad political issues and whatever else happened to cross their minds, included everyone, each with one equal vote: staff, board, Friday Folders, Thursday night layout crew, writers. Also hangers on, friends who stopped by the office to eat lunch, and various lost souls with no place else to go, like the strange young man, not at all bad looking, with cream-in-your-coffee colored skin, short, somewhat dusty dreadlocks, huge green eyes, and a sinuous walk, who showed up every day for weeks. He would sit at the front desk drawing and typing frantically and, in an attempt to be helpful, answering the phone and greeting visitors with friendly non sequiturs like, "Good afternoon. Do you like avocados?"—a phrase that was bandied about until it became our name for the *Advocate*: the *Avocado*. One Thursday night he shut himself in the bathroom and refused to come out. We'd accommodated him by running upstairs to the third-floor bathroom, which normally was used only by certain male staff for sexual assignations—and, Roberta claims, by her, too, when she was having her hot affair with Lucy Miner, the ad manager. Finally at 2 a.m., after we'd finished laying out the paper and were exhaustedly locking up, I banged on the door and pleaded with him, "Come out of there! We want to go home! We've been here all day!"

"So have I!" he yelled back.

Which shows that we all have our work to do. He got a vote too, when he wanted it.

This particular membership meeting had been called to discuss the announcement by Jearld Muldenhauer, the owner of the Glad Day gay bookstore that had recently opened across the hall from us, that he was having a large sign made for our street-level entrance. Membership meetings were either poorly attended and perfunctory or jammed and full of intrigue and high drama, and you could never predict exactly which way things would go, but this one was definitely headed toward the latter. We GCNers unanimously opposed a sign—because of the bullet holes, and people like avocado-boy, who no matter how sweet they were inevitably became a hindrance to getting work done. We were already the only listing under *Gay* in the telephone book, and some evenings we were busier than the Samaritans. And yet wasn't this anti-sign line just a bit inconsistent for a group whose basic principle was out-of-the-closet-and-into-the-streets? This contradiction had begun to give rise to a generalized desire for a major debate.

The meeting was just getting started when there was a commotion in the stairwell—a lot of banging and swearing. Everyone froze. Despite all our arguing, we were not a physically aggressive bunch. I was about to point out to Jearld, "See, this is exactly the problem!" when Mel burst in as though he'd been kicked over the threshold, red-faced and sweating, carrying a stick or some weapon-like thing he'd picked out of the trash. He leaned against the front desk to support himself and batted at the crowd of us with his stick a few times, pleased to see how we shrank from him.

"Miss Horne is drunk!" he declared.

Next to the front desk stood a large potted palm, the result of an advertising deal we'd made with a gay florist who couldn't pay his bills. The plant had become a sort of mascot, named by a meditative volunteer Sri Palmananda, and people occasionally hung ornaments from its fronds. Bellowing, Mel suddenly lunged at the palm and began whacking it with his stick. All I could think was *Call the police*—which was patently absurd, the police never came to the aid of the likes of us—and irrelevantly, a headline for the article when the whole ridiculous incident was all over: Man Attacks Plant; Terrifies Activists. A smell of leaves and dirt rose into the room.

Mike Riegle had joined the staff as office manager not long before, which is probably why he was still attending membership meetings, since later he avoided them and all meetings, and groups of any kind except the tangles of men he encountered on his nightly walk home, which took him through the Fenway Victory Gardens. He was of Mel's generation and class, and it was he who finally sighed, stood up, and crossed the room. Standing next to Mel as he flailed at the tree, Mike said in his slow deep voice, "Mel. You're ruining our plant. It's a shame."

"Get away from me, Mary," Mel panted.

"Oh, please," said Mike, ignoring the stick, putting a hand on Mel's shoulder. "What the hell are you doing? Let's go out and I'll buy you a drink."

Mel turned from Mike and swatted at the plant a few final times, but he kept missing it. The passion had suddenly left him. He dropped the stick and wiped his forehead with his hand. "Oh, awright," he said, glaring at the rest of us. "How'm I going to get down those goddamn stairs?"

Mike took his arm.

A few seconds later there was another commotion in the stairwell, and we could hear Mel shouting up to us, "Nelly faggots! Crazy diesel dykes!"

Having no experience with hysterical drunks, I was amazed by Mike's resourcefulness in offering to buy Mel a drink, which was the last thing that would have occurred to me. Mike appeared back in the office not long afterward, saying only, "I lost him." Shrugging his shoulders. He'd seen it before. I remember Mike also offering to call Mel a cab, as a possible alternative to a drink, but when I mentioned this to Mike once, he objected, insisting that he'd never in his life called a cab nor ever would—our discussion took place long before Mike got so sick with AIDS that he was forced to use cabs, which Medicaid would pay for under certain circumstances, and other forms of unpleasant transportation such as ambulances. So who knows how Mel found his way back to his apartment that night. I picture him passed out on a hard, unfamiliar sidewalk. Rain, mud. Eventually he picks himself up and trudges home.

Maybe Doug is there, and he cleans him up, puts him to bed. But probably not.

Mel didn't show up for the rest of the week. In the *GCN* features section I had once run an interview with counselors from the Homophile Alcoholism Treatment Service, and when I called them, they offered to come in and counsel the staff for free. They instructed us to allow Mel to return only under certain conditions: no coming in drunk, no drinking in the office, required daily attendance at AA. One slip, and he's fired. For counselors I thought they sounded harsh and unfeeling, but around the room the other staffers nodded. They had their own issues, it turned out— fathers, ex-lovers. "But he needs our help," I said.

"This is help," the counselors insisted. "You don't want to *enable* him to keep drinking, do you?"

This was a new concept for me. "I guess not," I said. "No."

No. Drunk, Mel was *not himself.* Neither he nor anyone else could predict what he would do next, and he could find himself anywhere, with anyone, doing anything. But, can a person *be* other than himself? Some philosophers claim that personality, the unique, abiding essence, is just a convenient fiction to get us through the day. It's not unlike our physical selves—whose cells are constantly multiplying, dying, and mutating, so scientists say we generate a completely new body every I don't know how many years. What we think is our unchanging essence is constantly being replaced with utterly different material. Consistency is an illusion. But the illusion is irresistible: all our manifestations share the same face, and after a while, I couldn't do other than blame sensitive Mel across the desk for the antics of wildman Mel with his stick.

"He may have to hit bottom," said the counselors.

"So we throw him out on the street with no job?" I asked.

"He knows what he has to do to keep his job. He can keep it if he wants."

Although I finally agreed to follow this course of action, in my heart I believed I knew it for what it was: abandonment. Abandonment of our gay brother, who was in deep trouble that he couldn't solve for himself. We couldn't solve it for him, either, that much I recognized. And I had no idea of what else to do. Insisting that Mel come to work sober was not unreasonable.

The staff decided that even though Richard, as managing editor, might seem to be the obvious person to say all this to Mel, about enabling and the conditions of his employment, he shouldn't be the one to do it. Mel thought Richard was a middle-class dick, who was always bugging him about working harder. He worked damn hard. With my desk next to Mel's as it was, and all the conversations we'd had, I decided I owed it to Mel to speak up. I'd endorsed the collective decision; I was now bound to carry it out. Someone else got the task of calling and asking him to come back to the office and meet with us.

He showed up, wan, punctual, silent. I expected him to be at least a little apologetic, but he wasn't at all, he was sullen as we tried to chat him up, which could have been embarrassment, could have been defiance, could have been distraction, as he tried to think back and figure out what he'd done. I took a deep breath, tried catch his eye, said my piece.

"Okay, okay, okay," he said, and rose to leave.

"Don't you have any questions or anything?" I asked.

"No," he said, finally meeting my eyes. "It's fine."

It was all very quick and dirty, as the saying goes. He might or might not show up to work again, but whatever happened, I realized, he and I wouldn't be having any more conversations across the desks. We had never been, would never be, friends. There was too much I didn't understand, about him, about everything.

He did return to work. And he may even have gone to a few AA meetings. Then one afternoon he produced a beer with lunch, and before Richard could make it across the room to get to him, because this time

Richard was going to confront him whether people wanted him to or not, Mel shouted, "You can't fire me, assholes. I quit," and left.

That was the last time I saw him.

Mel was murdered a year later, walking home from Chaps bar with Doug. Two kids jumped them and took "money, jewelry, and personal papers," according to "Former *GCN* Staffer Killed During Robbery," *GCN*, April 18, 1981—although this seems incredible. Money—after a night at the bar? Jewelry—maybe Doug's, he might have worn a gold chain. Personal papers—like credit cards? But Mel and Doug didn't have papers and credit cards; they were the kinds of people who didn't have a bank account and paid their bills with money orders, who couldn't always afford to keep the phone turned on. The article is written in idiotic hard-boiled prose and ends in a long, unnecessary riff quoting all sorts of officials and bystanders about when exactly the ambulance arrived, implying that there was some kind of homophobia going on with the emergency squad. It also says Mel was stabbed in the chest. Promptness wouldn't have saved him.

The article continues, "The assailants demanded money, and a struggle ensued." I once lived in an apartment where the quickest way home from the Star Market was by way of a dark tunnel under some train tracks. Whenever I started down the crumbling stairs I chanted to myself, "Drop the groceries. Drop the groceries and run. Throw down the groceries." I was afraid that if someone ever *assailed* me, my first impulse would be to hang onto my precious yogurt and carrots and laundry detergent. So I trained myself. Not Mel. He would hang on. He would mock the kids and shove them out of his way. He never had anything worth taking, and maybe he thought that should have protected him.

I say it was homophobia no matter how long the ambulance took. Mel was gay and he was murdered. No coincidence there.

A couple of sissies, it looks so easy. Then Mel goes nuts on them, and the threatening blade slips in. The kids run away fast, fast. Their blood pumping through their arteries, Mel's blood spraying onto the sidewalk. Mel collapses, Doug holds him, screaming for help.

No one gave chase. No one was ever arrested, or even sought.

Like it never happened. Like Mel had never lived among us in the first place. Except I have proof, a picture of him from the *GCN* photo file, marching with the banner, which he had conceived. I ran the picture on a page of reminiscences in the issue after the murder, but *GCN* published no follow-up news stories. By then, only Mike and I had worked with Mel. Our staff turnover was so fast—the jet-powered revolving door, Richard used to say. Even he, who'd been a fixture for so long, had left the paper by then for law school, and I had to put a call into him on the pay phone at school to tell him the terrible news.

Friends of Mel's—no one I knew—organized a memorial service at the Arlington Street Church. I went with Richard. Mel's service wasn't held in the big main sanctuary we were familiar with; instead we had to follow a series of hand-made signs to an obscure meeting room. Metal folding chairs had been set up in rows, and in the front of the room was a desk holding a record player like the one I'd brought to college, which closes up into a suitcase when you're done with it. On the turntable a Billie Holiday album was playing—one of the later ones. Some consider this period her most transcendent, and the fact that she had hardly any voice left beside the point. The speakers were tiny and the record worn and scratched. When the first side of the album ended, a man walked up, turned it over, and returned to his seat. People began shuffling in their chairs and coughing.

I felt a rising, claustrophobic panic. Would this be the whole program? Sitting in the basement listening to records? Something like that could go on forever. How would we know it was over and we could leave? Finally the man in charge of the record player stood up again. "This was Mel's favorite music," he said. "As you listen, if you have a memory of him or a thought you'd like to share, please feel free."

Richard, sitting next to me, groaned. "Don't ever do this to me," he said. "I want a choir and flowers and a real eulogy."

"Shh," I said.

"I'm serious. I'm leaving detailed instructions in my will in case you forget."

A few people spoke from the audience—neighbors, acquaintances, they all wished they'd known him better—with long intervals in between filled by Billie's voice. I wanted to contribute a memory and do my part to keep the service going, but I couldn't think of even one of our conversations. I couldn't picture Mel at all. His hair had been reddish, thinning, fading. But his eyes—were they blue or brown? The music didn't help; it only brought up my parents, jazz fans, playing Lady Day and Frank Sinatra on the hi-fi. They would dance around the living room, they would hold out their arms and offer to teach me the box step. I knew their eyes perfectly—my mother's round, sparsely lashed, green with gold flecks; my father's Slavic and slitty, deep brown. All I could remember about Mel was how he went wild, and I didn't want everyone else remembering him that way forever too.

Unlike me, Richard had come prepared. He'd brought a story Mel had written for *GCN* about his memories of Stonewall, or rather of Judy Garland, and of the transformations he'd witnessed in gay male culture, "Twenty Years of Changing Clothes." He stood and read it.

"Mel! You were my sister!" a man cried out. "I'll miss you, honey."

In the back of the room, a lesbian stood up. "Listen you guys," she said. "I knew Mel for twenty years. And I can tell you, Mel wouldn't have wanted this. Mel would've said, 'Go on out and have a beer!'"

Another voice: "Yeah, right on!"

"A beer, for Mel!"

Chairs scraped all around, and the mourners rushed out of the church.

Finally I could see Mel clearly, in our office, leaning back in his chair with his feet up on the gray metal desk, holding a can of beer, humming a song by Billie Holiday.

"Them that's got shall have. Them that's not shall lose," Mel crooned. "God bless the child that's got his own. That's got his own."

13

The Rage Warehouse

I knew I didn't want to leave the paper the way John Graczyk had. He had briefly been the *GCN* office manager, a blond, square-faced midwesterner with the beefy body and thick neck of a football player—except that John was a former monk. Actually, I guess he'd been a pre-monk, since he was in his early twenties, like the rest of us, and a recent graduate of some kind of monk seminary. I was never clear about the details, because he left *GCN* a few months after I started working there, and because I was shy of him, having no idea what to make of his history. This was before the lesbian nun craze of the eighties, when suddenly ex-contemplatives seemed to be everywhere, writing exposés about the cloistered life and their special friendships. John's background seemed unique and unfathomable. Had he worn a brown cowl and a rope around his waist? Did he even now retain Catholic beliefs such as transubstantiation?

I didn't feel I could ask him, although I had a Jew's prurience about these matters. A few years before, taking the train to New Jersey for the family Passover seder, I had sat next to a plainclothes nun. I wasn't hip at all to her post–Vatican II garb until she began to chat with me, since the only other nun I'd ever spoken to before that was the fascinating aunt of my childhood neighbors, about whom I used to badger them: "When is that bride coming to visit you again?" She had worn a white veil. I hadn't yet started kindergarten. On the train, I was carrying a book, *Sister Gin*, recently published by Daughters, a small feminist press that the author, June Arnold, had founded—how else were you going to get your experimental lesbian novel published?—and a turkey sandwich.

"Is your book about a nun?" the nun asked.

"No," I said, astonished at her interpretation of the title. "It's about a lesbian."

She was unfazed. From the nun memoirs that have been published since, I realize it wouldn't have been the first time she'd encountered a type like me. She might even have been one herself and known quite well what my book was about, having already read it. "Where are you going?" she asked.

"To visit my parents for Passover," I said. "But as you can see I'm not very religious, since I'm eating a sandwich." It was on a nice onion roll. Primitively, I was expecting the Lord to smite me. I felt like the *shtetl* Communists, who ate their mid-day meal of chicken basted in butter on Yom Kippur and afterward strolled through town, lighting up cigarettes as they passed the synagogue, bellies aching, eyes tearing. Before the ark, their fasting fathers swayed and beat their breasts.

"Because it has meat in it?" the nun asked, thinking perhaps of her own no longer required meatless Friday "fasts." Jews in no way consider eating fish to be fasting, maybe because to eat our fishes a person must have assiduously cultivated the taste for them—herring pickled raw with onions; gefilte fish balls floating in that clear jelly, into whose nature no one dares inquire too deeply, nor into the nature of the gefilte fish itself, slathering it with beet-colored horseradish. These concoctions of root vegetables and bottom-feeders are no fishsticks.

"No, bread," I explained. "It's forbidden. I should be eating matzo." The cracker of suffering. That's the theological difference right there: whether you forgo the protein or the carb.

John had occasionally alluded to wild sex among the monks. I imagined a medieval scene, with the cowls and ropes flying, all taking place in a suburb of Minneapolis. A couple of months after John had left his job, he stopped into the *GCN* office to talk to Richard.

"I had a nightmare about this place," said John. "I dreamed I burned it down with all of you in it."

From John's nightmare I learned: Quit before you get angry. Leave the party while you're still having a good time.

Except that it was already too late. Never in my life have I been so angry as I was at *GCN*. There's a sign on a building near MIT in Cambridge that says

METROPOLITAN STORAGE WAREHOUSE
FIRE PROOF

But from a certain, well-known spot on Mass. Ave., it reads

RAGE WAREHOUSE
IRE PROOF

I was approaching the point of needing to rent a cubicle in the Rage Ware-house. Because of things like this: Rob Schmieder, who was art director for a while when I was managing editor, accused me of mismanaging the paper's finances—what there were of them—because I had refused to give Larry Loffredo, the advertising manager, yet another advance on his com-mission. No, forget "mismanaging." He accused me—I can hardly write it even now—of stealing. His accusation didn't make much sense—I never understood how it was connected to Larry's request—and Rob was prob-ably just seizing a great opportunity to harass and intimidate me when Larry, with his characteristic combination of optimism and poor judg-ment, asked him to plead his case.

From that moment, I've known exactly what the expression *blow your top* means. I was so mad I felt as though fury were actually blasting out of the crown of my head in a shower of sparks, smoke pouring out of my ears, like in a Looney Tune. I *saw red*. I was *beside myself*. These sayings are simply literal. The experience was transcendent, in a way. I shrieked something at Rob, hardly aware of what I was doing, and rushed out of the office, down the stairs, and past the shoppers crowding the entrance to Filene's Basement and the gray-suited men of the Financial District.

Ishmael observes, "Let the most absent-minded of men be plunged in his deepest reveries—stand that man on his legs, set his feet a-going, and he will infallibly lead you to water." I don't know how long I stood at the filthy shore of the Boston Harbor, watching the iridescent ripples, realizing that at *GCN* I would never be able to do even one tiny thing right; and that this had nothing to do with my actual decisions, principles, intelligence, or character. It was enough merely to do—anything. Rob's accusation, and all those the preceded and followed it, was inevitable. If I *had* given the feck-less Larry his advance, the criticism would have been the same.

At the time, both my sister Priscilla and Richard were living in San

Francisco. Priscilla was going to San Francisco State and working as a cocktail waitress at the Cliff House, a tourist destination where from the bar, tended by my future brother-in-law, you could watch seals, dolphins, and even occasional whales cavorting in the bay. Richard was clerking at the Lesbian Rights Project (later the National Center for Lesbian Rights). Despite Northeastern's reputation for being so liberal that five years after graduation most of its alumni weren't even practicing law, Richard was only able to get credit for this project because of José Gomez, a student he knew at Harvard Law School. When Harvard initially refused to sanction José's gay internship, he wrote his dean a letter gently pointing out that neither he nor the law school administration would want to become involved in what he termed a "lengthy litigious dispute." We found the number of syllables in Jose's phrase tremendously satisfying and his argument bold, since we knew quite well, even if Harvard and Northeastern didn't, that the universities had nothing to fear from litigious gays. It wasn't until 1989 that Massachusetts became the second state in the country, after Wisconsin, to pass a gay rights law.

Richard had been sending me postcards and calling me on the phone to tell me what a blast he was having in San Francisco. I didn't quite want to know all the details, which I suspected involved frequent sexual encounters with short, bearded strangers (his favorite type) and drugs of unknown provenance—in addition of course to his exciting and worthy legal projects. He was staying in a sublet arranged for him by Harry Seng, who after quitting *GCN* had moved to the gay mecca in search of warmer weather and a husband. Harry was delighted when he heard that Richard was coming to stay for six months. He was constantly bemoaning his underemployment in the office of an insurance company he referred to as Miss Mutual, and what he said was the Bay Area's lack of an intellectual tradition, by which he meant the failure of any of the potential husbands he met to share his interest in rereading the novels of Henry James. But there were compensations for the daily grind in San Francisco in the fall of 1981, even for a man as choosy as Harry. The cruising areas were located in stunning parks filled with bright tropical flowers and palm trees, as gay men had wisely taken over some of the loveliest landscapes in the city. And although Harry's Catholic upbringing had left him wildly antireligious, he regularly worshiped at the Church of St. Priapus. (This is not a clever metaphor invented by me, but was an actual church, with unique services and observances.) But you didn't have to go anywhere special at all—there were hordes of gay men everywhere, greeting one another, catching eyes, holding hands in couples or even groups.

Personally I hadn't had a good night's sleep since the Thursday night, or actually Friday morning by the time the printer somehow tracked me down, to ask me what I wanted to do about the fact that our brand new art director on her first week on the job had designed a *17-page issue.*

The problem becomes immediately apparent if you imagine a sheet of paper. Now, fold it in half, and count its surfaces. Four, right? You will never in a million tries get five or three or any other number, and this rule of four and its multiples governs the overall design of any publication of any size, including newspapers. I admit I bore at least some of the responsibility for this idiotic mistake, since it was I who had conducted the blessing of the paper, a rite first instituted by Richard. At the end of Thursday night layout the volunteers and staff would gather around the light tables in a circle as the art director displayed each completed page to the group for its approval, pointing out the ads, the knockouts for the photographs, and other details. Once the paper was blessed, the art director had the additional chore of delivering it to the printer, while the rest of us were free to scatter into the night, to our homes or other destinations. On that particular Thursday, something hadn't seemed quite right to me, but page-by-page the paper hadn't looked any worse than usual. I told the printer—who was loudly making it clear that we were by far his most inept clients, not only in terms of basic skills and common sense but also of writing timely checks—to kill a page of letters to the editor. The subsequent pages would be numbered incorrectly, but that minor inconvenience to our readers, who had suffered so many, seemed preferable to a design that was physically impossible to produce.

After I hung up, I fell back onto the bed, eyes open, stiff as a board. Urv said rationally, "Go back to sleep, honey. You can't do anything about it now," but I was traumatized. I couldn't move, I couldn't sleep, and my mind was racing. The new art director quit the next day, in a huff, as though we were the ones who'd wronged her.

So I decided to take a few weeks' vacation, a sabbatical, and visit Richard and my sister in San Francisco. Richard was delighted that I'd finally stopped being so stubborn about working all the time—for some reason when he works day and night it's different—but Urvashi was furious. In her opinion, if I was going to relax and have fun for a change, I should do it someplace where she could be involved.

The terrible truth is that I was feeling increasingly disengaged from our relationship—as on the night the printer had called, only now it was all the time. My anxiety about everything that was going wrong at *GCN* was claiming more and more emotional territory, imperialistically colonizing one space after another that used to belong to something else. Urvashi had made me *chappatis* and treated me every day with love, desire, and affection, yet I barely noticed any more, even though after the Betsy/ Andrea debacle I had thought that all I wanted was for the girl I loved to love me back. Of course, Urvashi had her own preoccupations. In addition to law school, she had her collective household and their bulk purchases at the food co-op and their study group and their banner—LEFT FEMINIST LESBIANS REVOLT, lavender, of course, and decorated with all sorts of shells and tassels and sequins, which they carried off to every demonstration they could find—and rock and roll. Urv had a bass guitar that she dug out of her closet every once in a while, to sit in with a band she and some friends had put together, which operated under various names: Lezzie Fair, Church Bizarre, Surrender Dorothy. (Was it Surrender Dorothy that we were trying to see the night she and I and Richard were confronted by a bouncer who demanded we wait outside until the band finished setting up? "You have to let us in, we're lawyers!" Urv yelled, but he wasn't persuaded.) Some day she fully intended to learn to play.

Try as Urv did to draw me out of my funk and pull me along into her maelstrom of activities, I felt increasingly jaded. I claimed that everyone had a finite number of meetings she could attend in her life, and I was close to using up mine, so I sat on the back porch and smoked cigarettes during Urv's study groups and household conferences. I liked my individualistic little apartment. Although roommates came and went constantly from Urv's house, it never occurred to us to move in together. It simply wasn't done: we meant to be free and adventurous, ready to try anything that might present itself, not tied down and limited. Women had had enough of that! Urv and I were nonmonagamous, sort of. She, at least, slept with other women, especially former girlfriends from out of town, like Sue Metro, who looked eerily like me, with her dark hair and glasses. She lived in Rochester, and when she visited Boston she liked to play the hick in the big city: "Why is all the food in your kitchen brown?" she complained to Urvashi. "The bread. The spaghetti. Even the eggs." And Eliane, with her glamorous French accent, of which no one could understand a word. I was jealous, but I didn't admit it, since I didn't approve of jealousy. And because I felt so guilty that I'd turned out to be so inadequate.

While I was away, Urv sent me postcard after postcard, the most poignant, one she'd made from a black and white photograph of herself slouched in a chair, pouting darkly for the camera. It's a rare photograph of her wearing her thick glasses instead of her contact lenses, and I immediately understood its message: "I miss you and I care for nothing; I am reduced to wearing my glasses." She might be lying in bed wheezing with asthma, unable to talk or do her law school homework or leave the house, which meant she would be *home* every Sunday morning when her mother called to berate her in Hindi for turning out so incredibly badly as to be a lesbian. Actually, in those calls her mother spoke a universal language. Or no, maybe Urv was so angry at me for abandoning her that she had found some other girl to run around with and was whooping it up every night. I didn't know for sure what state Urv was in, because her postcard just had a lot of x's, o's, and hearts on the back, and a Mousie-style ad she'd posted and then clipped from the *GCN* classifieds—she knew I would avoid reading the paper—that said, francophilically for some reason, "*Amy chere amie*, we miss you we miss you."

Meanwhile, San Francisco was just as great as Richard had said it would be. I was nobody there, with nothing in particular to do. Staying in a corner of my sister's living room, my main responsibilities in life were to fold up the couch in the morning, cook a few meals, run a helpful errand or two. I drifted along in formless days, occasionally walking around a neighborhood I'd heard of—the Castro, the Mission, Berkeley, Golden Gate Park. I went to City Lights bookstore, to see the place that had published the small, square edition of *Howl and Other Poems* that had been a cherished part of my library since high school, and to the clothing stores on Haight Street. My sister and I drove across the Golden Gate Bridge to Tiburon; Richard and Harry and I went on expeditions south to Santa Cruz and north to Bolinas. Occasionally I called someone, like the *GCN* writer with whom I had lunch and then tagged along with afterward as she picked up a few items for a party she was hosting that evening: a rubber sheet and a couple of S-hooks. She didn't invite me to the party, I suppose for the same reason that a few months earlier, the review I had written of a lesbian sex manual had inspired a cartoon from the artist I asked to illustrate it that pictured an Amy-character smiling tentatively as several women, one winking seductively at her, repair to the bedroom. My avatar is wearing a "Hi! My Name Is _____!" pin. The caption reads, "Your first orgy?"

In 1981 the lesbian movement was being wracked by the great sex wars—although according to the anti-sex side, they were *not* against sex. They were just against yucky sex—any activity involving the use of implements, substances, costumes, reading material, or recording devices, not to mention multiple partners, simultaneously or successively. Our new ad manager, Sherry Edwards, who had replaced Larry when he finally admitted there was no way he could make a living at the job, was experimenting with color Xerox art—a new medium—the subject of which was usually her and her two girlfriends in bed together. Created by manipulating the images over and over, the final pictures were abstract, but you could make out a tangle of legs if you knew where to look, and the colors were the same acid blues and magentas that highlighted Sherry's hair. As *GCN's* managing editor I counted automatically among the sexual liberationists, which was a lucky break for me, since as much as I wished to be dashing and outrageous, my actual behavior was closer to the ideals of the other side. When Andrea visited San Francisco, she came back claiming to have patronized a dyke bathhouse. Only one problem: the women were actually bathing. No, that's a joke. The women were doing just what the men did in their bathhouses—having wild sex with strangers. When Andrea returned to uptight old Boston, she immediately flew all the characters in Random Lust out to San Francisco for a vacation based on her discovery. But when I was in San Francisco and took myself out to a lesbian bar to look for an adventure, my longest conversation of the evening was with a woman wearing a leather cowboy hat, who could plausibly have been sitting on her stool since 1955.

But it was all fine. I'd walk outside and see palm trees, as if on a desert island, and eucalyptus, which I'd never even heard of before. The houses were multicolored. San Francisco looked like no city I'd ever been to. I'd meet up with Richard and Harry in the evenings at Harry's neighborhood gay bar—a concept that fascinated me. The gay bars I'd known existed specifically to take you *out* of your neighborhood, to a place where you were unlikely to run into your cousin or boss or the churchgoing couple from next door.

One day the three of us took a bus to the end of the line and hiked down a cliff to a little beach on the cold Pacific. Land's End was a sometime gay cruising area, and while we sat shivering on the rocks, Pan stumbled out of a clump of trees. He had a furry chest and legs, and little horns peeking out of his curly hair. His face was gray, his eyes bloodshot, and he seemed to have lost his pipes. Halloween had been the night before. Richard and I had gone to a party at the home of a former Thursday volunteer, for which Richard had dressed in drag for the first time in his life. I could tell it was an important rite of passage for him in his identity as a gay man, although to depict the woman he had chosen—Sandra Day O'Connor, then newly appointed to the Supreme Court—he didn't need to wear falsies or heels or show off his legs. We found a black graduation robe at a secondhand clothing store in the Mission, and a friend of Harry's did Richard's wig and makeup, although he would have liked a more glamorous character to work with. A drag queen requires an entourage, so it didn't matter that I wasn't wearing a witty outfit myself. People in costume crowded the streets and buses, rang up groceries, and served dinner in fancy restaurants. In San Francisco in the early eighties, Halloween was a major civil celebration that expressed the city's essence—playful, sexy, bent on confounding all assumptions about character, gender, or even species, as with Pan.

But eventually, of course, the costume loses its charm: The pins and basting holding it together give way, your makeup rubs off, your wig gets pushed askew, your feet develop blisters from the crazy shoes, and you finally give up and put your street clothes back on. You're back in character, which is comfortable and familiar, or perhaps I should say ill-fitting and stifling. The famous San Francisco fog lifts, and the plane, which has been grounded, offering a temporary reprieve until the weather clears, takes off.

Back at the office I told everyone that my sabbatical had re-energized me, but that was a big fat lie. After a single morning—no, an hour; no, not even that, just walking in the door—despair and exhaustion enveloped me. The weight of all the decisions made, or not made, during the past four years; the sides taken in disputes; the confusing personal, political, and expedient alliances; the ever-present financial crisis; the coming and going of staff: I just didn't see how I could continue, bumbling around and doing everything wrong. Bill-paying had become a matter of determining which creditors would stop providing some essential service, such as telephones or printing, and which could be held off for another week. It was harder and harder to find writers and other volunteers—even the number of Friday Folders was decreasing. And no matter what we published, the only topic anyone ever seemed to want to discuss in our letters page was boylove. Instead of learning from experience, I seemed to myself to be getting less resourceful the longer I was editor. But neither could I figure out how to stop. I couldn't imagine anyone wanting to take my place. And even if such a person did turn up, I didn't know how I would explain to her what I did, although I was busy from morning until night.

I was constantly terrified that I would finally be exposed as an incompetent fraud. I believed I'd been skating along on luck and a few good friends like Richard to advise me. And my luck and the good advice and my few ideas had run out. I could no longer figure out what to do about yet another letter to the editor about intergenerational sex, yet another drop in subscriptions, yet another failed fund-raiser, yet another departing ad manager. Or my inability to feel anything, even toward Urvashi, whom I loved and who loved me.

Mornings I lay in bed with her and said, "Why am I unhappy? I don't know what to do."

"I know, baby," she said.

When she pulled me toward her, I felt like cardboard.

Leaving the paper, which for so long had been inconceivable, began to seem necessary. Countless others had done it before me, and countless others would follow. I have no recollection of how I managed to announce it, but at a certain point in the spring, everyone knew.

My combined goodbye-*GCN*/early-thirtieth-birthday party was held at the Summer Palace.

Or was it the Winter Palace? Anyway, it was one of the mansions up on Fort Hill, with a little cupola on top, although you couldn't go into the cupola, because of the dire state of the upper floors and roof. It belonged to Ian Johnson and Kruk Kruekel. Ian was one of the founders of the paper, a former managing editor, and he would occasionally invite Richard and me to dinner in the half-renovated kitchen and hold forth on the current state of the paper, and how it had changed since he had worked there.

A secret collection, which I now realize was probably masterminded by Urvashi, trying to cheer me up, was taken up among the staff and the volunteers to buy me a fabulous gift: a leather jacket. I had a leather jacket, of course—you had to. We once ran an ad in the *GCN* classifieds from a group of women seeking a roommate for their collective household in which they described themselves as "3 Dykes and One Leather Jacket," which suggested so poignant a story—did they post a rotation wheel on the refrigerator similar to the one used to assign the cleaning chores?—that the phrase was eventually used by a local writer as the title of her novel. My jacket was secondhand. Although the label said "genuine leather," it had always had a plasticky look about it. On one expedition to New York, Richard took a picture of me wearing my leather jacket and dark sunglasses, with the Statue of Liberty in the background. On the back of the print he gave me he'd written a caption: "Who's that revolutionary?" But for a few years now, it had had a big tear in one sleeve where I'd caught it on a chain-link fence. Usually, I manage to discount praise and thanks as formulaic and basically insincere expressions of courtesy or obligation, but even I couldn't quite dismiss the check I was given: The size of it and the number of contributions involved were too large. I was flabbergasted.

Urvashi and others were dying to come shopping with me, but I wanted to pick out the jacket by myself—it was going to take me into the next part of my life. Leather jackets fell into one of two categories: motorcycle or aviator. Motorcycle jackets, with their hard black leather and elaborate zippers and buckles, seemed way too butch and complicated for me, so I leaned toward aviator. Andrea had had one that I'd always admired. At Helen's Leather on Charles Street, I found a kind of stylized version—it wasn't as bulky as aviator jackets tended to be, but small and fitted. It was made from soft leather with a taffeta lining and knitted cuffs and waistband—which was somewhat of a problem, but I resolved that in my new life, I would tuck in my shirts.

When I appeared in it for the first time at my party, the pretty jacket disappointed everyone who had contributed to it. Sherry and her girlfriends used to wear matching motorcycle jackets when they went out together, which nicely complemented Sherry's electric blue hair, and she expressed everyone's misgivings when she saw me: "It's *brown?*" she exclaimed, before she could stop herself. What a cop-out.

14

The Fire

The seven-alarm fire that incinerated the *GCN* offices at 22 Bromfield Street early on Wednesday morning, July 7, 1982, a date I vowed never to forget and in fact never have, was so hot that it melted every piece of plastic in the place, including the refrigerator and the telephones. It vaporized our ever-evolving wall collage, not to mention the walls themselves, right down to the charred studs. Our salvaged desks and homemade light tables and plugged-up waxers and broken-down typewriters and four-drawer homo-file and obsolete addressograph machine were reduced from junk to stinking, waterlogged rubble. The Charles Ash article index was turned to ash indeed, for the fiery winds to whirl through the downtown Boston streets, past the Locke-Ober restaurant, where Charles used to lunch in the days before women were admitted. (Or at least this is what I had always assumed, until I learned in a recent conversation with Libby that in fact, Charles's index ended up with the gay history project, the cards browned but readable and even, as project volunteers compile their own index, useful.)

I should have been peripheral to the whole terrible scene, since I'd quit the paper, and my name had appeared on the masthead for the final time several weeks before, but because of a little kink in the gay grapevine I was the first *GCN*-associated person to arrive at the fire. A onetime board member, Ken Westhassel, who'd been gone long enough—a few months?— that he didn't know anyone on the current staff, had in desperation contacted me after receiving an early morning phone call from a guy he'd met at Dignity, the gay Catholic group. (Ken's membership in Dignity was

VOL. 10, NO. 1   July 17 1982   60¢

Gay Community News

THE WEEKLY FOR LESBIANS AND GAY MALES

BIPAD: 65498

GCN BURNS

photo by Marie Favorito

GCN BURNT OUT

probably the reason he was a onetime rather than current board member, since such religious groups were generally scorned by us at *GCN* as examples of mass, delusional internalized homophobia—*gays : church : blacks : Ku Klux Klan.*) Ken's friend, the closeted chaplain of the Boston Fire Department, had recognized the significance of the address 22 Bromfield Street when the alarm came in. I said goodbye to Ken, rushed out of the house, and jumped onto the subway, which was then delayed in the tunnel between stations. A smell of burning rubber permeated the car, a common enough occurrence, but as I sat there in the dark, no explanation forthcoming beyond the usual incomprehensible squawks from the train's public-address system, I wondered whether the whole city was in flames above us.

Bromfield Street was barricaded with fire trucks and police cars and filthy white canvas hoses snaking everywhere. Smoke and flames were shooting unbelievably out of the roof of our building. Helicopters pound-ed overhead. Running around like an ant whose hill has been flooded, I screamed at the firemen, "Mike! Mike! Mike might be in there!" Our office manager often spent the night, when he stayed out late and didn't feel like trekking all the way home. Or at least, that's what he told people. But Mike's favorite cruising spots were closer to his apartment than they were to *GCN*; convenience had nothing to do with why he virtually lived in the office. He'd built four walls around his desk, and that was where he kept his special coffee cup, never washed; his sleeping bag; his toothbrush; his manual typewriter for writing letters to gay prisoners; his books and papers and the *GCN* checkbook. He didn't believe in materialism, but he believed in office supplies, and his desk drawers were full of pens, large-size paperclips (he didn't trust the small ones), and Post-its, his favorite twentieth-century invention (years later, when AIDS made him sick and forgetful, he showed me a Post-it he thought would amuse me—stuck to the bedside table in his apartment, which he'd finally resorted to living in, it reminded him, "Wear underpants"). Occasionally he would fish out a blue packet of foul Gauloise cigarettes and dole out one to himself and one to me, sitting in the dimness in the desk chair with the missing wheel that he kept for visitors. The walls of Mike's cubicle were covered even more densely than those in the rest of the office, with his hand-lettered quotes from Foucault, pictures cut out from magazines of humpy guys and trees and birds and other manifestations of nature, the crafts projects that the prisoners sent him as gifts, and anything else that happened to catch his scavenger eye. At a certain point, probably after he'd gotten mugged by some trick and had disappeared from the office for a day or two, he had entrusted me with his home phone number, and on the day of the fire I used it for the first time, calling him from the pay phone on the corner. No answer. It was insanely early in the morning. Where else would he be, but on his pallet on the office floor?

"No one's in the building," a fireman yelled back at me. He was absolutely confident, but I didn't see how he could know. The artists who lived illegally in the top floor studios were milling around on the sidewalk, stunned, watching as their life's work went up in smoke. "They say everyone's accounted for."

"But they're not! They're not! Mike sleeps in there! On the second floor! You have to check!"

At that moment, Mike turned the corner, wearing his usual frayed denim shirt, ancient knapsack, and green Victory Garden baseball cap—a premium from the local public television station, which produced a gardening show by that name. The cap represented to Mike his favorite Boston landmark and cruising area, the Fenway Victory Gardens. He may have stopped to check out the early morning scene on his way to work, or, equally likely, never left the previous evening—I never found out exactly where he'd been. "Hey," he said. "What's all this?"

I grabbed him. "I thought you were upstairs," I said. "I thought you were dead."

He looked amused. In the confusion surrounding us, he hadn't yet grasped the fire's enormity. "Not yet," he said. "Still hanging in."

As the morning wore on, a crowd gathered: staff and volunteers from *GCN* and *FagRag* and Jearld from the Glad Day gay book store across the hall—with whom we later got into a big fight about whether his shop was a community service worthy of a cut of the post-fire donations we were receiving or a profit-making business venture that could just as well fend for itself. People stopped by because they'd seen the fire on the TV news—the first story some had ever seen there with any relevance to their gay existence—or stumbled across it on their way to work, as the blocked streets threw the downtown into chaos. With the building burning before our eyes, it felt like a moment for decisive action, but there was nothing we could do but gawk. Hug. Cry.

Finally the smoke cleared, and the firemen stowed their equipment and maneuvered their ungainly trucks out of the narrow street. Alone in the sudden silence, those of us standing on the sidewalk were hit by a collective adrenaline rush that didn't subside for weeks, enabling superhuman feats of work and organization. We were like crash survivors who find themselves suddenly able to pick up cars. The paper didn't miss a single issue. *Gay Community News*, Volume 10, Number 1, was only eight pages long, but it came out that Friday, two days after the fire. The editorial apologized, with frenetic understatement, "It's not the usual paper . . . but then, it wasn't the usual week. We're used to an occasional rowdy visitor and funny noises on the phone, but *really* who could be prepared for this?" Encountering the same spirit, a reader recounted in the letters column a few weeks later:

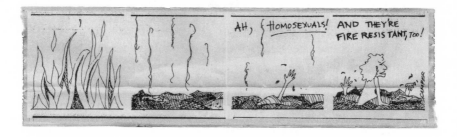

When I called the other day to complain about having to pay postage-due on my subscription (I recently moved), someone answered after many rings and said wearily, "Things are kind of hectic around here." I thought to myself, well, half the staff is probably on vacation and the other half is enjoying the summer weather, and what can I expect from a community group? Today I received your issue and found out why things are kinda hectic.

A rare five-column headline was splashed across the front page—FIRE DE-STROYS GCN OFFICE—and underneath, "A Personal Account: Down but Not Defeated." Pictures throughout showed groups of us standing around in shock, details of the burned offices, the art director dangling a melted telephone out the broken front window, and there I am, talking to Chris Guilfoy and Maida Tilchen. We're standing in front of a fire truck: Ladder 29. Since the fire happened on a Wednesday, some of the copy, the ads, and standard items like the back-page calendar had already been sent to the printer. For weeks, the calendar would continue to invite volunteers to help lay out the paper on Thursdays and mail it out on Fridays, location: "22 Bromfield St. (near Park St. T stop)."

John Ward generously invited us to work in his office, since as a lawyer he actually had an office to offer, in contrast to most of the gay groups around town, which met at people's houses or cheap restaurants—or at *GCN.* The office was small, since John spent most of his billable hours on things like trying to persuade the IRS to recognize *GCN* as a nonprofit organization (that effort had finally succeeded when, instead of submitting an application for *Gay Community News,* Inc., Richard suggested calling ourselves the Bromfield Street Educational Foundation, which after the fire became a memorial of sorts), defending men who had been caught having sex with each other at highway rest stops, helping divorced lesbians get visitation rights with their kids, springing transvestite hustlers from jail, and similar disreputable and impoverished cases. By the end of the day, we had set up our crisis headquarters. It was so crowded and busy, with us running around and holding press conferences and yelling into telephones among lawyers and assistants trying to get their own work done, that at one point I participated in a meeting sitting on the floor under a conference table, while a second meeting took place on the surface overhead.

That was when I learned the word *accelerant*. It bounced out of the meeting on the top of the table, which was with agents from the Bureau of Alcohol, Tobacco and Firearms. I'd never heard of that before, either. The agents' shoes were shiny and black.

Of course the *GCN* fire was arson. The ATF guys theorized that fire had been started in the back of the building, probably with an accelerant lobbed into the *FagRag* office—the FagRaggers took a lot of pride in this. Suspects abounded from the start, and none has ever been decisively proven guilty or innocent, including:

1. The police. In the months before the fire, they had been spending more and more time patrolling the fearsome criminal environs of the Boston Public Library basement men's room, greeting the patrons and arresting any who responded or even made eye contact. It figured that Mike had been caught up in this tearoom sting, and, since he was a pivotal member of both the *GCN* and *FagRag* collectives, the groups decided to hold a joint demonstration. Mitzel got hold of a bullhorn and led the chants: "Abolish the vice squad! Turn the building into a women's health center!"—which has always seemed to me oddly generous of him, since he certainly had no interest in women's health, or women generally, and in fact often wrote things that were absurdly sexist in his *GCN* articles, exciting letters for weeks afterward. After the demo, someone had Krazy-Glued our building's door lock, an act of vandalism—or warning?—that was blamed on the vice squad, or alternatively, by some, on:

2. Organized criminals. This complicated theory went back to David Brill and his articles investigating the unsolved murder of the hustler Dale Barbre. I know I won't get this right, but I think the idea was that the same sinister persons who had murdered Brill, or forced

him to commit suicide, because he had been on the verge of discovering the motive, method, and perpetrator of Barbre's murder, had now torched the office to destroy Brill's last remaining files and the shocking evidence contained therein. Or perhaps it was just about the ownership of certain bars and bathhouses around town, against whom the paper had occasionally fulminated because of their exploitative prices, unsanitary environments, and unwillingness to spend money on advertising, not to mention the many nights when we'd found ourselves dateless at closing time.

3. The landlord. Although to the untrained eye our building could hardly have been more nondescript, it apparently was a unique example of some sort of hideous factory architecture, and shortly before the fire, the city had declared it historic. Desperate to gut the place and find tenants who would pay more and timelier rent, the landlord torched it. For months after the fire, *GCN* ran articles about baffling financial manipulations performed by the building's management company—such as the transfer of the building's ownership to a "straw" for one dollar. The management company never returned our reporter's calls, freeing him to speculate in any direction he pleased. There certainly *seemed* to be a scurrilous connection between these transactions and the fire, but exactly what the point of them was, the articles never explained. I have to say that a mark against this theory is that the upper floors of the building, in an increasingly valuable neighborhood, remain boarded up to this day. Every once in a while, when I have an errand downtown, I walk down Bromfield Street to check. The last time Richard visited Boston, I showed him too. No one has ever moved in.

4. A random bigot unaffiliated with the vice squad, organized criminals, or our landlord—this simplistic theory had about as much appeal and credibility to us as the Warren Commission's conclusion that Lee Harvey Oswald was a lone gunman.

5. A wacked-out gay person—even more distasteful, but it's undeniable that we received letters daily from readers who claimed we'd unforgivably angered and offended them.

Several years after the *GCN* fire, the *Boston Globe* exposed a conspiracy of disgruntled firemen who had set fires in buildings all over the city, including at 22 Bromfield Street, with the confused notion that this would make the people of Boston realize the firemen's value and create a public demand for increasing their pay. But this still doesn't explain, to my satisfaction, our fire, since no one has yet delved into the question of how the arsonists chose particular targets. Why was our obscure office building among them? Does it not make sense that firemen who would turn to setting fires would also be available to act as agents for corrupt police, organized criminals, greedy landlords, bigots, crazies, etc., etc.?

Once I arrived at the fire, I couldn't leave—for days, literally, except to run home for clean underwear or a sandwich, since one of the first things we decided was to keep a round-the-clock vigil over what was left of the building. If I stopped to think about it, I wasn't sure what we were supposed to be looking for, what we would do if a suspicious character showed up, or for that matter, what further harm anyone could do, but the situation was so scary—someone, somewhere, hating us enough to threaten not only our project but our lives—that it was impossible not to get caught up in the general paranoia (and, as the hippies used to say, it's not paranoia if they're really out to get you.)

I signed up for the midnight shift, with Mike. In the alley at the side of the building, we sat on beach chairs with frayed plastic webbing— donated perhaps by some thoughtful person who surmised that all of our chairs had burned up. Various nocturnal characters came by to show their support. A boy with a guitar, who played us a number of his original folksongs. A woman with a pleasant, gap-toothed smile leading an asthmatic German shepherd. She claimed to be an old friend of Mike's and an avid volunteer and to know me, too, although I'd seen neither her nor her dog ever before, and haven't since. Brian McNaught, the mayor's recently appointed liaison to the gay community, rode by in a police car. None of these people seemed to be likely repeat-arsonists. Brian stuck his head out the passenger-side window and called out to us to go home and let the mayor and the police do the job of securing the building. But how could we could trust that, given our list of suspects and the fact that *GCN* had been running articles for months relentlessly and no doubt gratuitously attacking both the do-nothing mayor and his sell-out liaison? It seemed clear that we would need to do our own protecting.

I suppose it's predictable that after a while people became restless with sitting outside the building, listening to folksingers and playing with dogs. They wanted to go in. It became irresistible, the urge to check out the situation for ourselves, rather than blindly trusting the authorities. How big had the fire been, exactly? How much damage could one fire really do? It got harder and harder to believe that we'd seen the building burning right in front of our eyes. (I wouldn't trust my own memories of it for a minute, were it not for such evidence as the photo of me and Ladder 29.) Ever obedient, I was inclined to follow the police instructions to stay away. The building was clearly dangerous, and I am not physically courageous. But eventually peer pressure and curiosity outweighed my fear.

We snuck in. Creeping around with a flashlight, you had to leap across the floor boards and hope you didn't crash through a hole. Walls, desks, file cabinets—just about everything was burned black and soaking wet. Electrical cables and insulation hung down from the ceiling.

When Mike, with his love of the worthless, the damaged, and the hopeless cause, saw all this he became obsessed with trying to rescue our stuff. Volunteers attracted to his urgency and sense of purpose formed a brigade, handing file drawers and bundles of messed up back issues down the stairs and out to the street. Others hauled them over to the basement of the Arlington Street Church, which let us use the space to spread out the papers, books, magazines, photos, and newspapers to dry. Desperately, Mike gave additional stacks to people to take home and hang on their clotheslines or lay out on their porches—he'd heard that sunlight would kill bacteria and preserve the documents. But paper is fragile, especially newsprint, and most of it crumbled almost immediately to dust.

There were a few neat souvenirs, like the melted telephones. And an entire carton of bright *GCN* T-shirts—red, pink, purple, orange—now charred around the edges and transformed into dickies and halters. We'd been promoting the shirts for months, with ads using strips of photo-booth pictures of *GCN* staffers and volunteers making kissy faces and wearing funny hats or, in one case, a scary black leather mask with zippers for eyes. The ads were headlined, *"Don't be a FASHION VICTIM!"* marking a new era of sorts at the paper, as some of the more recently hired, punkier staff people thought of themselves as trendsetters rather than as homo misfits who enjoyed giving themselves asymmetrical haircuts. Richard can't be the only person who salvaged one of the burned shirts to frame and hang in his living room. And Bob Andrews actually wore one, to the emergency community meeting at the Arlington Street Church that we called for the Monday after the fire. The style was to razor off your T-shirt sleeves and collar—but burnt off turned out to be even better, especially since Bob looked so great in his shirt, his muscles bulging out of the missing sleeves, his midriff showing through the fragile fabric. The shirt he'd picked out was turquoise, which brought out the bright blue of his eyes. For some reason the rest of us were wearing colored bandannas tied around our upper arms, like the ones gay men wore in their back pockets to show they were available for certain sexual practices—the bars gave out cards listing the various colors and their meanings. My bandanna, which Urvashi had given me and which I still have, was lavender and meant either "drag" or "group sex," depending on whose key you consulted; I wasn't much interested in either, but I liked the color and wearing a present from my girlfriend.

Cindy Patton, who had succeeded me as managing editor and now found herself in charge of a hideous disaster, had probably started the bandanna-around-the-biceps fad—her biceps were one of her vanities. Wearing our bandannas, she and I had our heads together talking and laughing when a *GCN* photographer snapped a picture that I'll never live down with Urvashi, who would probably claim to this day that it proves beyond any doubt that my thing with Cindy started that night, when I sat down in the pew next to her, and that Cindy was the reason I broke up with Urvashi several months later. But I swear I had no thoughts of Cindy nor of anyone else that night—nothing, until well *after* I broke up with Urv, in the midst of one of those conversations full of silences, when each of us said at one point, "Maybe this just isn't working . . ." Usually we fell into each other's arms and agreed to try again. This time I answered impulsively, "No maybe it's not," and was immediately overcome with a terrible feeling of misery and panic, since I realized I was making an irrevocably awful decision. Urv phoned me every morning for weeks to berate me for it, and I would imagine her voice echoing down the hallways of the law firm where she was clerking and think, "They will never hire a lesbian again."

The meeting at the church was huge, nearly nine hundred people. Everyone on the program had been given a particular role—presenting the arson theories or the pitch for money or the *FagRag* perspective, and I'd been appointed to give the political analysis at the climactic moment. As I rose to speak, several microphones were thrust in my face to catch my words. The old *GCN* banner—conceived by Mel Horne, sewn by Raymond Hopkins—hung on the pulpit behind me, burnt and tattered and water-damaged but still surviving, still legible, just like old *GCN* itself. I concluded,

> I was very upset last week to find myself misquoted in the *Boston Globe* as having said, "We are destroyed." *We* are not destroyed; just our office is. It never occurred to me or anyone else at 22 Bromfield Street that our voices would be silenced by the fire. Even while I stood there watching the flames shooting out of the roof, I knew that *GCN* would publish on Friday as always. *Gay Community News* has been able to publish weekly since 1973 because of the courage and support of the lesbian and gay community, and as long as we continue to have that, we will not be destroyed.

Pretty inspiring stuff. The audience cheered and wept, and I was proud to have found the words to express what we all were feeling at that moment of crisis.

But now I confess: the *Globe* did not misquote me. I have no doubt that I uttered every word it said I did, and even at the time, deep down, I knew my peroration was in bad faith. I had said, "We are destroyed," and I was right. *GCN* was never the same after the fire.

Maybe that's fine. Times change, and even without the fire, the paper would have had to change with them. It could never have lasted as long as it did if it had clung to nostalgias like mine—and perhaps all of us who worked there have a secret tendency to think of our particular era as the paper's golden age. And it's not as though the ideals changed, or people's dedication to them—keeping the paper going after the fire was surely the most difficult thing any *GCN* staff ever accomplished. In fact, many of the activists who were afterward indelibly associated with *GCN*, to the extent of being called a "gay mafia," because they went on to run practically every gay organization in the country—the National Gay and Lesbian Task Force, the Lambda Legal Defense Fund, gay community centers, the AIDS groups that were springing up around the country—were those who served on the staff after the fire. Including Richard, who rejoined after he finished law school.

Not to endorse feng shui or any other such mystical systems, but I've

GayCommunityNews

Vol. 10, No. 1 ————————(617) 426-4469———————— ©GCN, 1982 ———————— July 17 1982

FIRE DESTROYS *GCN* OFFICE
Arson Suspected in Seven-Alarm Blaze

By Larry Goldsmith

BOSTON, July 7—A seven-alarm fire believed to be the work of arsonists swept through the Bromfield Street offices of *Gay Community News*, *Fag Rag*, and Glad Day Bookstore early this morning, leaving little but ashes and debris in its path. The fire, which struck on the eve of *GCN's* tenth year of publication, also destroyed several artists' lofts on the upper floors of the building. Two firefighters were reported injured during the attempt to extinguish the blaze, and several persons in the lofts had to be rescued from fire escapes.

At a hastily-arranged afternoon press conference, *GCN* Managing Editor Cindy Patton said that "although the fire department says the fire was of indeterminate origin, we believe it started as a result of arson — arson for profit or arson for political vengeance."

"In recent months, while Boston's vice squad has been out raiding gay bars, there have been an increasing number of attacks on gay men and lesbians in the streets," Patton explained. "The attacks, raids, and, we believe, this fire, are symptoms of a worsening climate of homophobia, racism, anti-semitism and sexism."

Patton and other members of the *GCN* staff said it was too early to decide who might be responsible for setting the fire. The paper had received no threats warning it of the fire.

The fire gutted both sides of the *GCN* office, which is divided by a brick fire wall. Office furniture and equipment such as desks, chairs and typewriters were destroyed or severely damaged. The entire inventory of *Fag Rag* and *GCN* back issues, including some now-rare issues, was devoured by the flames. Across the hall, Glad Day Bookstore suffered water and smoke damage.

Files maintained in metal file cabinets and desk drawers largely survived the heat and flames, although most sustained moderate damage from smoke and water. Much of the news files, photo files, advertising and financial records appears to be salvageable.

Confidential mailing lists are maintained at a separate location and are safe, and all confidential files have been removed to a safer location.

Firefighters at the scene told *GCN* staff members the fire started near the rear windows of the offices where the *Fag Rag* collective sublets a small space. Pieces of molten metal and glass found near the windows testified to the intensity of the blaze.

The rear windows of the office open onto a fire escape which provides access to an adjoining alley. In September of 1978, shortly after an appearance in Boston by anti-gay crusader Anita Bryant, vandals broke through the same windows and ransacked the *GCN* office. Although protective bars had since been installed in those windows, it appears that arsonists may have climbed the fire escape and tossed an incendiary device between the bars.

Not far from the window, a hole was burned into the floor, possibly where an incendiary device had landed.

Ironically, the fire escape leading to the rear of the office underwent extensive repair about two

Continued on page 4

photo by Ellen Shub

News Commentary

photo by Ellen Shub

A Personal Account:
Down but not Defeated

By Scott Brookie

The news spread quickly: most of the *GCN* staff members heard that their workplace had been reduced to ashes even before the fire was put out. That information didn't reach *GCN* through any official channels, however. No fire marshal notified the managing editor, there was no call from the landlord. Instead, a member of the fire department, who is also a member of Dignity (the gay Catholic group) heard the alarm come in. Recognizing the address, he called a friend of his, who called someone from *GCN*, who called someone else. . . .

"We really *are* everywhere," mused *GCN's* attorney Cindy Rizzo as she heard that story rezo as she heard that story recounted. It was one of the many little moments that helped lift and dissipate the heavy cloud of doom and helplessness which had begun the day.

It was lunch hour in the financial district by the time firefighters were rolling up the hoses. So many people, after gaping at the blackened windows, approached Promotions Manager Maxine Feldman with offers of help ("Total strangers!" exclaimed Maxine) that someone — another stranger — had to give her a notebook to write down their names.

Support and assistance were immediate and plentiful. By midmorning, three publications had offered *GCN* free workspace. The printer would give us credit; the typesetter wouldn't charge. By midafternoon, two local bars had offered to put on benefits and another benefit was in the works for New York. Plenty more will be necessary.

Those who had headed downtown to the what-do-we-do-now meeting wondering if the paper could still exist soon found that the relevant question, in fact, was whether we could get together an eight-page or a twelve-page issue in one day. "Nobody's giving in, nobody's defeated, nobody's even

particularly depressed," remarked News Editor David Morris. "*GCN* burned down this morning," announced another staffer to a new arrival. She allowed him perhaps five seconds, then continued, "Now, pick up your jaw and get to work."

The tremendous amount of work to be done masked (perhaps sublimated is more accurate) a widespread sense of shock, but it surfaced periodically. "I didn't know whether to cry or throw up when I saw it," recalled one volunteer to local reporter Larry Goldsmith as they walked away, "so I didn't do either."

"I know," remarked Larry. "It's like someone died." They walked on in silence for awhile. "Oh, my pink hat!" remembered the first person in an agonized

realization. "The one with the netting on the front, that said 'press.' It was on my desk."

"See?" sighed Larry. "This is going to go on for months."

There were some memorable sights: members of the fire department, their work finished, thumbing through the smoky and waterlogged remains of Glad Day bookstore's more explicit offerings, pointing and gawking. The aggressive television news reporter who, having grilled *GCN*, *Fag Rag* and Glad Day representatives, was now on the phone to the cops: "What do you mean, no comment?" she demanded. "In my entire career as a reporter you've never had no comment. The gay community says they don't trust you. Doesn't that

Continued on page 4

photo by Ellen Shub

always wondered whether the problem was the new office. Obviously the staff couldn't continue meeting under lawyers' desks for very long. Luckily, for the first and only time in the paper's history an actual benefactor turned up. A closeted gay man, he was inspired by our situation to come out at least enough to offer *GCN* free temporary space in a downtown building owned by his family. One floor was empty, scheduled for remodeling, and he said *GCN* could use it for six weeks or so, until the contractors were ready to start work. Eventually we overstayed our welcome— not on purpose, but just because it was so difficult to find an affordable, permanent home, and our benefactor thus found his first venture into gay politics totally exasperating. He was about to forcibly evict us when we discovered the former Cinderella School of Beauty on Tremont Street, across from the Boston Common.

It looked like it had been designed by the world's tackiest drag queen. The walls of several of the rooms were papered with a custom-made, repeating image of the blonde, page-boyed princess, and one of the main jobs that had to be done before *GCN* could move in was to haul away all the huge, conehead-type hairdryers (some of which are probably still sitting in David Peterson's basement). The Bromfield Street office had consisted of two large rooms, forcing everyone to interact constantly and to listen in on one another's telephone calls; but in the warren of rooms that was the Cinderella School, everyone was closed off in her own private space. The corrupted collective reached its most extreme, with everyone insisting on her political righteousness and her prerogative, no, her *obligation* to the future of the movement to do whatever she saw fit. Plots and shifting alliances and accusations dominated every interaction—the politics were as thick as those in the court of the Sun King or even the English department of a small college. Everyone on the staff grew to hate everyone else—at an entirely different magnitude than ever before, beyond anything even the Rage Warehouse could contain. Richard and I were having dinner together one night at his apartment, and he'd been abusing various staff people so venomously for stupidity and incompetence and causing the downfall of *GCN* that finally I couldn't stand it and cried out, "Stop it! Stop it! Leave! It's ruining you!" and went home. But he didn't leave, not for many months.

While the building was still in flames, after Mike appeared, I had made another call from the booth across the street, to Richard, whom I called with a lot of bad news in those years—Brill's death, Mel's. On the day of the fire he once again wasn't in Boston because of a personal disaster; he was on Long Island, visiting his mother. He could do nothing about the fire from there, but I wanted him to know. I wanted him to be part of it with me.

Richard was visiting his mother because his father had died suddenly the previous March. Richard had called me then and asked me to come over to his apartment—but not right away. "Wait a few hours," he'd said. When I arrived, he seemed to have finished with any grief he felt and had turned instead to berating his father for carrying an inadequate amount of life insurance. "How could he have been so totally underinsured? He was a lawyer! What about my mother?"

Richard displays a few belongings of his father's in his apartment: a strange painting in the style of Jackson Pollock, a map of Ireland, an antique clock. Although his anger has mellowed, Richard rarely speaks of him, and there are no pictures of him among the photos and cards propped all over the bookshelves—the wedding picture in the silver frame is of Richard's mother alone, its focal point the sweeping train of her dress. I met J. Richard Burns only once. To me, he looked like Daniel Patrick Moynihan—but maybe that was just his big Irish face and outsized presence. As I've discovered often happens when one relative is a drunk or a madman, as the dinner guest I was assigned to talk to him, providing a brief respite for the family circle. In our conversation, he managed to list the name of every Jew he'd ever known.

My call woke Richard up. "The office is burning down! I'm standing here on Bromfield Street, and smoke is pouring out the roof!"

I don't think he quite believed me. It was so early—maybe he thought it was a bad dream.

After his father's funeral, Richard had finished his law school semester, but then taken a leave for the summer term. On Long Island, his mother gave him his father's old Chevy Caprice, which he drove up to Boston the weekend after the fire, making it back in time to speak at the meeting at the Arlington Street Church. For the rest of the summer he and I traveled around together—to the Berkshires, to Provincetown, back to Long Island—we couldn't afford to go far, and we were limited to destinations where friends or family didn't mind putting us up for free. Richard would drive, and I would sit beside him, getting us lost.

Gay Community News was never the same after the fire, but neither was anything else, and if only it were the new office—but the office was nothing, really. On the roof of our new building, on a cool evening, *GCN* held a little office-warming party. Bob Andrews and I stood looking out over the Boston Common, holding plastic cups of white wine as he told me a strange story about a guy he knew—our age, really cute. He'd caught pneumonia and died *in a week*.

AIDS didn't even have a name yet.

So much for those piles of books Richard and I had imagined, the scholarly tomes, the kiss-and-tells. After the scourges of the eighties and nineties there are simply not that many of us still available with an interest and an unclouded mind. Believe me, I've asked around, but the results of my research have been disappointing. Lots of generalizations, few stories, no dates or names or scrapbooks. And some people seem embarrassed or even embittered—by our earnestness, our youth, the times. I'm not embarrassed, or at least not much. But I don't have any scrapbooks either, and I've never been able to keep much of a journal. I never thought I'd need them. I used to be able instantly to visualize any article on any subject we'd published during my tenure and to tell you not only what was on that week's cover but what page the article was on and even in which quadrant. That's all gone, though, so my spotty and only somewhat accurate recollections will have to do.

As Ishmael says, on the last page of *Moby Dick*, "And I only am escaped alone to tell thee."

Except I'm luckier than Ish. His solitary fate is not mine. No lesbian ever entirely gives up her ex-lovers. And Richard and I are still friends, too. When I visit him in New York City, he makes up the living room couch, sets out a bath towel and a glass of water, and dims the lights, and as I crawl under the blankets he says, "Good night, Aim. Do you have everything you need?"

"Yes, of course," I say. "Good night."

He still reads the *New York Times*, although he claims less obsessively, so that he falls asleep some nights having merely glanced at the headlines. Even so, he's the only person I know who has the knack of reading a newspaper at the beach, sprawled in his sand-chair, the pages luffing noisily in his face. It's absolutely his favorite thing, to settle into what we atavistically call the DMZ between the men's and the women's zones of the gay beach in Provincetown, coated with sunscreen, a white T-shirt wrapped kafiyyah-like around his head, behind the tent of the news. Beside him, my Roberta and Urv's lover Kate set up the Scrabble board—Roberta already preparing to curse her loss, because she inevitably succumbs to a beautiful word, while Kate is our queen of the triple word score.

So many of the people I've named in this story are gone—Dave Stryker and David Brill and Mel Horne and Mike Riegle and Walta Borawski and Raymond Hopkins and Ian Johnson and Nancy Walker and Gregory Howe and Bob Andrews and Eric Rofes—and so many others whose names I haven't mentioned. Who would've thought they'd be the ones watching over us—the Ancestors, so to speak. Except I don't believe in the afterlife. I'm still mad about that AIDS movie that ends with all the dead friends rematerializing at Fire Island Pines. In my story, it's the living who gather on the beach, friends and friends-of-friends and lovers and exes and rivals and children and dogs. Surrounding Richard and Roberta and Kate we lounge on the sand, on towels and a print bedspread Urvashi brought back from India—her mother speaks more kindly to her these days. The children run down to the water. Spurred on by Urv, her nose and lips smeared white with zinc, the rest of us get involved in another favorite pastime: arguing politics. Tomorrow we'll have work to do.

ACKNOWLEDGMENTS

Writers often complain about the solitariness of their art, but I don't think I'd ever get a word on paper without my writing partners, Anita Diamant and Stephen McCauley, and their encouragement, dinners, wonderful talk—their friendship. They've patiently read and reread my manuscripts, always providing wise counsel and innumerable commas.

Hans Johnson insisted that other people would so be interested in my old stories.

Years ago when I first tried writing about my time at *GCN* in the form of a (failed) novel, Urvashi Vaid said, "Wait a minute. Where our real names? And why am I not in here more?" I am grateful to Urv, Kate Clinton, Richard Burns, Roberta Stone and the rest of my gay family for generously pushing me to tell the truth as I saw it, even when it was not as they did.

Betsy Smith talked through many ideas and inspired many insights, often while speedwalking around Fresh Pond or in phone conversations from her bathtub.

The following people submitted to interviews, answered random questions, and shared their memories: Michael Bronski, Richard Burns, Brian Cummings, Tom Huth, Neil Miller, the late and sorely missed Eric Rofes, Will (Harry) Seng, Charley Shively, Roberta Stone, Urvashi Vaid, and Nancy Wechsler. Libby Bouvier, queen of The History Project, which documents GLBT Boston, generously gave her time on many weekends to help me poke around the *GCN* archives, photo file, and other records. The following people also provided help finding photos and other sources:

Richard Burns, Marie Favorito, Susan Fleischmann, John Kyper, David Peterson, Ellen Shub, and Rich Wandel, archivist at New York's Lesbian, Gay, Bisexual and Transgender Community Center. All errors, distortions, exaggerations, memory lapses, lacunae, and crackpot misinterpretations are of course mine.

Bruce Wilcox and the staff at University of Massachusetts Press have been gracious, enthusiastic, generous with praise, tolerant of my anxieties, and sparing with their blue pencils—they're the best. Janice Irvine is nothing less than the ideal Reader.

The love, wisdom, integrity and *menshlichkeit* of my parents, Sigmund and Serena Hoffman, is more important to me with every precious year. I have always tried to follow in their footsteps, although they sometimes, no doubt rightly, wondered about my poor sense of direction. I treasure the conversation and wit of my sister Priscilla Morrissey and my other loving brothers, sisters, inlaws, outlaws, nieces, and nephews.

As well as being a true doll and a dear, wonderful friend, Richard Burns has been a generous and uncomplaining subject and an ever-patient and discerning reader.

Finally, where would I be without Roberta Stone, my lover, girlfriend, companion of my heart, computer guru, official photographer, guardian of the scriptorium, and spouse-in-Massachusetts (and some day the world, babe).